3 2 AUG 2011

Securing Appropriate Education Provision *for* Children *with* Autism Spectrum Disorders

Securing Appropriate Education Provision *for* Children *with* Autism Spectrum Disorders

A GUIDE FOR PARENTS AND PROFESSIONALS

Allison Hope-West

Foreword by Dr Glenys Jones

Jessica Kingsley Publishers
London and Philadelphia

First published in 2011
by Jessica Kingsley Publishers
116 Pentonville Road
London N1 9JB, UK
and
400 Market Street, Suite 400
Philadelphia, PA 19106, USA
www.jkp.com

Library of Congress Cataloging in Publication Data
Hope-West, Allison.
  Securing appropriate education for children with autism spectrum disorders : a guide for
parents and professionals / Allison Hope-West ; foreword by Glenys Jones.
     p. cm.
  Includes bibliographical references and index.
  ISBN 978-1-84905-153-8 (alk. paper)
  1. Autistic children--Education--United States. 2.   Autistic youth--Education--United
States. 3. Autism spectrum disorders 4. Inclusive education--United States. I. Title.
  LC4718.H66 2010
  371.94--dc22

                                         2010020755

British Library Cataloguing in Publication Data
A CIP catalogue record for this book is available from the British Library

ISBN 978 1 84905 153 8

Printed and bound in Great Britain by
MPG Books Group

In memory of my mother
Marie, who made all
of her children feel that
they were invincible

Acknowledgements

I would like to start by thanking all of the children and families that I have had the privilege of working with. Their journeys have not always been easy, and yet they continue to pick themselves up, dust themselves off and get on with it, often in the face of real adversity. They have been a total inspiration to me and have taught me never to give up. I am deeply indebted to you all.

I would like to thank my husband Martin and daughter Stacey who have supported me and encouraged me to write this book in the first place. I would like to thank Dr Glenys Jones for her help in editing and proof reading and for writing the Foreword. I would also like to acknowledge the support that I have received from tutors at the University of Birmingham.

Finally a huge thank you to my good friend Evelyn Ashford who wrote the chapter about her son Jasper. Thanks for the late-night chats and the suggestions that have given me ongoing commitment to completing the book. You have helped me more than you will ever know. Thanks also to Jasper for his contribution of 'his side of the story'.

The cover picture is by Steven Reed, a wonderful young man who taught me far more than I taught him.

For the purpose of this book I will refer to 'your child', rather than 'a child known to you'. I will use this as a term for both parents and professionals. The word 'child' is used to describe children of both genders. For reasons of convenience, both boys and girls are referred to using the pronouns 'he' and 'him'.

Contents

Foreword

This is an ambitious book which covers a wide range of topics concerning educational provision for children on the autism spectrum. When parents are given a diagnosis of autism or Asperger Syndrome, they want to know what that means, how they can help and also what type of school their child might attend. This book aims to give ideas to parents on all these questions. It also has sections for parents prior to diagnosis – for those parents who are concerned about their child's development or behaviour and want to explore why this might be. So there are chapters on what the signs of autism are and how a diagnosis might be made involving professionals in health, education and social care.

The book begins with a very moving account from a mother whose son has Asperger Syndrome. This is followed by reflections from her son, Jasper, on what he thought of the various schools he went to. The family is known to Allison Hope-West, the author, and it is apparent that much of what appears in this book has its origins in what this family experienced. Their journey through the diagnostic and education systems was not easy or positive, but happily Jasper now enjoys his current school and is progressing well.

The hope is that the ideas and information provided in this book – and in the many resources and websites provided within it and in the Useful Websites section at the end – will enable parents and children with autism spectrum disorder (ASD) in the future to have a much smoother journey and at less emotional and financial cost. We have learned a great deal on how to create effective educational environments for children on the autism spectrum and it is the case that many mainstream, special and specialist schools are now much better at understanding and teaching these children than they were in the past. Children on the autism spectrum can be very different in terms of their intellectual ability and the degree to which autism affects them, so a range of educational provision needs to be made by local authorities.

Some children will succeed in mainstream schools with little additional support, whilst others will find a typical mainstream classroom too challenging and will require different provision. At present, alternative provision which children with ASD might attend include units and bases within mainstream schools, special schools for children with learning difficulties, specialist schools for children with autism or Asperger Syndrome and home education. There is no template which allows parents and professionals to decide easily what type of provision is most appropriate for a particular child. As Allison points out, parents need to visit a range of schools in their own local authority and make a judgement about which school is most likely to suit their child, using the very detailed knowledge they have about their son or daughter. They need to consider on the basis of their past experience how their child will respond to the physical and sensory environment, the other children on roll and the demands made in terms of the curriculum and the social aspects of the school. Open and informed discussions with professionals involved with the child can then together lead to a decision as to which school will be most appropriate. If disagreements do occur between parents and professionals, then this book gives parents guidance on people within the local authority who might help and organisations who can advise on what to do.

Allison has stressed the importance of focusing on areas where the child experiences success and to build activities and interests into the day that they find rewarding. It is the case that the literature in the past has tended to list all the areas of difficulty a child with ASD might have. This can make depressing reading for parents and the child himself. Whilst not making light of the very real difficulties that children and adults on the autism spectrum and their families can face, there does need to be a balance between a focus on their difficulties and the needs arising and an acknowledgement of their successes and different way of looking at and acting on the world. Books like this which aim to inform parents on how they and others can make the best decisions to support their child effectively should lead to positive outcomes for all concerned – the child, the parents and the brothers and sisters, whose needs are sometimes left out of the literature, but which Allison has also discussed.

Dr Glenys Jones, Lecturer in Autism,
School of Education, University of Birmingham
April 2010

Introduction

This book was written following the journey of one mother's attempt to secure appropriate educational provision for her autistic son. I have been involved with the education and placement of young people with autism for nearly 15 years and have worked with hundreds of families; however, with this particular family I was party to the whole process, from attempting to secure a diagnosis to finally securing an appropriate educational placement. I was shocked and stunned to find the barriers that were raised to block this process, and the lack of understanding of some professionals involved. The family's journey will be outlined in this book, and I am sure that it will strike a familiar chord for those families and professionals who have had experience of engagement with a variety of agencies. I hope that it will also give some guidance to parents and professionals who are at the beginning of this process, and will help to identify some of the likely issues that you may have to deal with.

My experience working in Local Authority (LA) maintained schools, independent specialist residential provision and within the LA have given me opportunities to explore many aspects relating to the identification, diagnosis and placement of young people with autistic spectrum disorder (ASD), as well as an understanding of special educational needs (SEN) law and the special educational needs and disability tribunal (SEND, formerly SENDIST) process. For the purposes of this book, the term 'autism spectrum disorder' is used to cover both Asperger syndrome (AS) and autism.

It may be that you have already secured a diagnosis for your child, in which case the chapters on securing appropriate educational provision and your legal rights may help. It may be that you are concerned about the possibility that your child has an undiagnosed ASD and are struggling to know where to get help. There are chapters covering routes to diagnosis and approaches which may help.

The cause of autism is unclear; however, there is a strong genetic component. It is a spectrum disorder, which means that children on the autism spectrum can be very different from each other in terms of their abilities, skills, personality and understanding. The needs and provision made for two children can therefore be very different. Many young people on the autistic spectrum cope reasonably well in primary educational settings, whereby they have one teacher for all subjects and teaching tends to happen in the same room. Problems often occur during the transition to secondary educational provision, whereby a pupil may have a different teacher for each subject, and may have to negotiate moving from one room or area to another. The organisation of books, kit and homework can also pose issues which may lead to isolation, anxiety and trauma.

There would appear to be a significant increase in prevalence (epidemiology) of people with ASD although there is little clear data available to support this. An unpublished report was cited as suggesting that it may be as high as 1 in 38 children. This report by Baron-Cohen *et al.* has since been published in The British Journal of Psychiatry (2009) and its full contents do not suggest that the figure is as high as this. It is widely accepted that the incidence of autism is four times higher in boys, and there are various theories that outline why this may be the case. There is, however, agreement that the number of people with ASD being diagnosed has increased. With this in mind, it is therefore likely that meeting the educational needs of this group of children would involve a vast shift in the amount and types of provision available. At first glance this would appear to be the case, with mainstream schools and LA special schools developing ways and systems of supporting these young people. However, even with reorganisation, many schools cannot support the government's targets for higher achievement as well as truly meeting educational need.

A significant number of students with an ASD have their educational needs met at their local mainstream school. The government's inclusion agenda has led, in some cases, to better training for staff in schools and to a greater understanding of the condition. Many mainstream and special schools now provide specific provision for young people with an ASD and therapeutic support is available on site. However, this will not address the complex and unique educational and social needs of a small number of students with an ASD.

Mainstream schools may be unhappy to have a population of pupils with special needs as this can affect performance (league) tables. These markers of achievement do not measure social outcomes or well-being in any significant form. This, along with a lack of understanding, training, effectively differentiated curriculum (that is, a learning programme which is broadly based on the National Curriculum (NC) but developed in such a way as to meet individual need), modified environment, access to therapeutic support and whole-school awareness can lead to young people with an ASD becoming highly anxious and placement breaking down very rapidly.

The government's agenda has shifted from integration to inclusion; however, what this means in real terms has not been clearly outlined. It would appear that inclusion in mainstream schools for some is by proximity alone, usually within a unit base where some pupils receive their education away from the main body of the school for much of the time. Other establishments offer full inclusion, sometimes with some support from a teaching assistant. Some are trained and work well but others may have no specific training in ASD and may be left to do their own research as to how to work effectively with a complex and often anxious young person.

There are a number of independent specialist schools across the country catering for more complex young people with ASD ranging from those who have severe learning difficulties (SLD) as a result of their autism to those who fall into the gifted and talented (G and T) range of ability. These specialist establishments are known as 'out of county placements', even if the child is resident in the same county. The decision for parents and professionals to start looking for out of county placements is rarely taken lightly, and often marks a breakdown in the current placement. This can be a lonely and difficult time for families, which can be exacerbated by a lack of available information and lack of support.

There are many organisations which may be able to help you find appropriate schooling and support in this process. It is vitally important that there is clarity surrounding what individual schools can offer as it can be easy to be dazzled and impressed with the location and environment of some out of county placements. This book provides a checklist of what to look for when reading Office for Standards in Education (Ofsted) reports and viewing provision, and the types of questions to ask.

There is also a huge number of support groups and local autism societies available to join, and it is likely that there will be one in your area. These groups can offer a great deal of information from parents who have been in the same situation, and are able to offer advice and guidance. The National Autistic Society (NAS) website (see Useful Websites section) can provide details of groups in your locality as well as offering a helpline, training for parents and internet social groups for young people.

The choice of educational provision is vast. Chapter 6 outlines the various types of school available both locally and nationally. All LA special schools and most out of county provision will require that your child has a Statement of SEN written by the LA. The process of securing a Statement from the LA is outlined in Chapter 10, as is content outlining specific educational needs and provision to meet those needs.

All LAs have an agenda to reduce the number of out of county placements and therefore their spend, as this type of provision tends to be very expensive. They are keen to spend the money saved on improving the schools and services within their own LA. Some authorities have developed their own provision to a level whereby young people with an ASD can truly flourish, through detailed planning and employment of autism-specific officers, teachers and teaching assistants to advise, train and mentor staff. Some have produced excellent guidance for schools wanting to become more inclusive and training DVDs are now widely available to all LA schools. Obviously there is a huge cost implication to this type of development, which has precluded some smaller authorities from tackling this issue with any vigour. There is no easy answer, and budgets are often overspent to the extent that hard decisions have to be made about which children are provided with the most expensive resources.

Mainstream schools have been tasked with developing more inclusive practice, with special schools increasingly being asked to provide outreach services to aid in this process. LAs have been charged with reducing the budget which is spent on out of county placements for young people with special needs, and the number of special schools has reduced significantly as disability-specific schools have merged with other special schools to create provision which caters for a much wider and more diverse range of SEN. Many agencies involved in the provision of education for students with SEN have found it increasingly difficult to provide individualised tailored programmes which truly meet often very complex needs because of this lack of specialism. This is a situation that is not going to change overnight and Ofsted have recently stated that at the present time they do not believe a major review of SEN is necessary.

I have spoken to a number of parents of children with an ASD about their experiences of mainstream, special and autism-specific provision and the response has been incredibly mixed. Some parents feel that their children have a greater opportunity to develop social skills when educated in a mainstream school alongside non autistic peers. Some commented on the skills of the special educational needs coordinator (SENCO) in ensuring that the curriculum was differentiated appropriately (changed to make accessible) and that behaviour modification plans were in place and understood. Parents who were happy with mainstream education spoke very highly of the way in which individual schools had responded and modified their approached, training, curriculum, environment and whole-school policies and practice to meet the needs of young people with an ASD.

Other parents were not so generous in their response, stating that their child was left simply to 'cope' and struggle through processes and systems which did not suit his needs at all. Many complained of the lack of understanding and training, as well as the lack of differentiation to the curriculum. Some talked about frequently being called to come and get their child who was upset or not engaging, as well as exclusions being issued which were not properly documented or conducted in line with the school's policy. Many also complained that inclusion actually amounted to exclusion, with few adjustments being made to meet the needs of their child.

Parents who had children in special schools appeared to be happier with the arrangement than those with children in mainstream education. They felt that staff understood their child better and that they made better progress with important things such as communication and development of social skills. They did, however, feel that the peer group was not always appropriate and that their children witnessed too many children displaying bad behaviour.

The final group of parents who had children in autism-specific schools largely felt that this was the best environment for their child. They felt that staff had a really good understanding of their child and his condition and that learning was based around this. Some made comments about a lack of resources and shabby buildings but felt that this was a small price to pay. Some did comment, however, that they worried about the amount of structure in the school and how their child would adjust when he moved on. The range of provision reflects the range of individual needs, and 'one size' does not fit all. Try and find the school that is most able to meet your child's unique needs.

Recently the Autism Bill (2009) was published as an Act and this is likely to have significant implications for young people with autism. This is the first piece of autism-specific legislation and outlines the need for LAs to be accountable in law to provide support to all young people with autism, including those with Asperger Syndrome. It will be interesting to see what this means in practice.

This book is not intended to be exhaustive; rather it may point you in the right direction and unpick the maze of legal jargon surrounding SEN issues. The internet is also a great resource, with many sites dedicated to helping and advising parents and professionals. This book cannot cover in detail every issue that you may have; however, it is hoped that the information contained within it will lead you to further resources that may be of use.

KEY POINTS

- Problems experienced by a child with an ASD can become especially evident during or after transition to secondary educational provision but this is not always the case.

- The prevalence of ASD is approximately 1:100 (ratio of boys to girls is approximately 4:1).

- Many children with an ASD have their educational needs met in a mainstream maintained school; however, for some children more specialist education is required.

- Some authorities have developed autism-specific educational provision which can be very effective for some children.

Chapter 1

~~~~~~~~~

Jasper's Story

This account was written by my dear friend Evelyn Ashford and charts her journey with her son Jasper and their experience of the SEN system.

Through my journey I have not only come to believe in the power of the individual to make a difference, but also in the value of each of us as individuals. My son has taught me this. I am privileged to be the mother of Jasper, a wonderful and unique person who has Asperger's in his life and who has touched the lives of many others along the way.

I was a successful, career-focused designer in my early 30s when the alarm on my biological clock finally got stuck. Overnight I turned into someone who hung around in the baby aisle in the supermarket so that I could sniff the talcum powder. Not too long after that I was proud to feel my bump kicking strongly, full of life and giving me new hope in mine. I had had my ups and downs and I knew that this child would change my life and give me purpose. I didn't have any idea just how true that would turn out to be!

On the day he was born I was in a particularly excitable mood; I had several contractions whilst shopping for Sunday dinner. At home I prepared the meal, having more contractions, keeping an eye on the roast potatoes, and being told by his dad, who had previous personal experience of childbirth, that it would be 'ages yet – possibly a day or two'.

Ten minutes later, when the head appeared, I screamed like a banshee at him to get the car, and gave birth eight minutes after arriving at the hospital. 'A drive through,' we called it.

I had a bath and put on some makeup, but was quite put out to be told to get back into bed as I was staying overnight. I felt no pain, only excitement, and I couldn't sleep at all. I just sat and stared at him in awe with tears rolling down my face, all night. That was my first major bipolar experience.

Shortly after his birth I was alone with this beautiful and mysterious package that obviously hadn't read Penelope Leach's book on childcare. He had screaming night terrors, which had me running down to the all-night NHS drop-in centre on a regular basis (usually with us both in tears). They had no real idea what caused it, possibly an ear infection, and they prescribed antibiotics repeatedly.

He didn't sleep through the night until he was four, which drove me nearly demented. He spoke in a garbled language which, I was told, 'only I could understand'. He crawled, stood and walked at all of the expected stages, but had an odd ability to complete difficult jigsaw puzzles at a rate of knots. On his third Christmas he threw together his very complicated Harry Potter LEGO® train set accurately, in minutes, without looking at the instructions, much to the amazement of our guests!

When his speech did begin to improve at around the age of four he appeared to 'read' bill boards out loud, though I still can't quite believe that myself. By then he had started to make three-dimensional models from paper by drawing exploded plans of trains and cars which he would fix together with sticky tape, forming perfectly detailed scaled replicas of his favourite story characters, all without the use of a ruler.

I now know that many children on the autistic spectrum have great difficulty with toileting and bowel problems. We were very lucky that for Jasper this was not the case. In fact I kept him in nappies until he was dry overnight and then one day introduced him to the potty, which he then continued to use without mishaps.

He was a very happy child who laughed constantly and was very self-occupied in his play. At nursery they remarked upon his apparent inability or lack of desire to play with the other children, which worried me slightly. These comments began to extend to his 'high pain threshold' following a few bumps, his lack of danger awareness and the fact that they still didn't seem to be able to understand his 'speech'.

He was an August birth, which meant that he was the baby of the class when he started school. That didn't help. Only a few weeks into his first term it was clear that something was seriously wrong. He would either be in floods of tears when I collected him from school, or, on a good day, would run into my arms as if to escape from something awful. They said that he was 'having trouble settling in' and 'throwing tantrums'. They questioned his home life and whether I disciplined him enough. I had several meetings with one particular teacher who made me feel completely incompetent. So I increased the level of discipline at home; this only made us both unhappy and finally I began research on the internet into the possibility that there may be an explanation for some of his unusual behaviour. The only thing I could find which matched some, but not all, of it was autism. This terrified me; I only hoped that I truly was a bad parent as maybe this was something that I could cure.

I requested a Statutory Assessment but was refused. A good friend who acted as nanny for us at home while I continued to work and who was previously employed at his nursery was allowed to go into school to help. This only highlighted the lack of understanding on the part of the staff, who didn't have her unique knowledge of Jasper and the time to dedicate on a one-to-one basis. Jasper responded well to her and was fine at home but simply couldn't manage in a large group. He would continue to have meltdowns when things went wrong, which escalated if not managed correctly.

Then one day a member of staff uttered the phrase which I will never forget: 'I've worked with children who have autism and believe me – your son has a problem, but it's not autism.' This was such a kick in the teeth. I immediately went back to the computer, the library and the bookshops and read everything I could on every syndrome known to man. I believed he was wrong. I paid for two private assessments from educational psychologists with the highest qualifications so that I could be sure. They both had entirely opposing views on how to 'embrace' or 'deal with' the undeniable fact my son had high-functioning autism (HFA).

I called a meeting to discuss this with a group of his teachers and, to be fair, some of them had tried to find out more about autism; this was in their own time and they had the best intentions. However, by this point they had been trying to 'train' him to sit on a square of red carpet when he was unruly or when he 'wandered'. This was a torturous punishment for someone who was later to be diagnosed with dyspraxia, as he could not concentrate whilst holding one position for too long. On my way into the meeting I glanced through the window of his classroom to see him rolled up in a foetal position under a table with his hands over his ears and sobbing. They said that they may be able to get him a few hours a week on a one-to-one basis with an assistant who would have no specific training in special needs let alone autism. The following day, using a template letter which I found on the IPSEA (Independent Parental Special Education Advice) website, I went into school and handed them my request to take responsibility for my child's education.

Home educating was an interesting experience. Jasper learned quickly and enjoyed it enormously. It gave me a different perspective on education and the way in which convention leads us to accept age-defined expectations of achievement. As an ex-interior designer I did a lovely job of converting our lounge into a school room. Jasper accurately painted the flags of about 20 different countries in our geography lesson to decorate the walls. We made the solar system to decorate the ceiling, and I bought a piano and a trampoline. Unfortunately all of these events were really taking their toll on me and the manic phase of my bipolar condition reappeared. I was as yet undiagnosed, but I couldn't give up my responsibility so I had to start down the road of our first tribunal to get him into what I hoped would be a special school.

Meanwhile, I found a fabulous home school centre which provided group tutoring on an occasional basis to support families like ours. It was a great blend of all ages and abilities, and it taught me that our system, which supports the majority, does not work for everyone and contradicts the natural mix of age groups within a family. The social aspect and the environment were perfect for him, and I have very fond memories of seeing all of the kids playing in the woods or building cardboard robots together. It was a private school, which by this time I could not afford, and they were clear that they did not have the expertise to challenge and support him academically. Jasper's time there gave me the space I needed and some of the emotional support to see me through; but those who really kept me going were my loyal and long-suffering friends, always there to make sure that I had eaten and that I was never alone when I was most afraid.

I read 10 to 15 books a day, returning them each morning to the library in carrier bags, I wrote endless letters to councillors and the media to highlight the problems we had encountered and I waded through the paperwork and details involved in trying to ensure that my child would receive the educational support he needed. By this time I was underweight and my hair was falling out in handfuls. Mania is a weird and wonderful thing. It can be a very useful illness to have, but it can also make you lose touch with reality. I opened a jewellery shop which ultimately failed, converted part of a house which I had rented out into a hairdressers, repeatedly mortgaged our own house and lost it all in legal fees, assessment costs, alternative business plans in an attempt to survive and frivolous attempts to cheer myself up.

I found a special school who said that they could meet Jasper's needs and sank the last of my savings into the mortgage of a house nearby so that we were in the catchment area. It was still a battle to get him in; the attitude of the local authority was very adversarial, at times truly intimidating, but finally we won the tribunal, or rather they backed down the day before the hearing. They held out just long enough for us to lose almost everything in the fight.

The relief was short-lived though. Jasper would come home covered in bruises. The special gluten- and dairy-free diet, which had worked amazingly well in helping him regain his connectivity and calm, was continually ignored by staff who would give him a biscuit or sweets to coax him into cooperating. When I discussed the qualifications of the teachers it appeared that they too had very little specific training in autism, and when I mentioned to the head teacher that I would be looking for another specialist school I was told that she could not support me.

Mania, as I said, is a wonderful thing! With the help and advice of Allison I scanned the pages of every directory of schools throughout the country. After telephoning or visiting in the region of 300 schools and poor Jasper having had three trials at potential placements which failed abysmally, we were almost on our last legs when I came across a new list and a school that really seemed to fit.

Now just the small matter of a good Statement! His previous one, which I had naively accepted, was deeply flawed. The use of the terms 'should have access to' and 'approximately' should have read 'won't get'. This is a binding contract – and should be entered into in the same way as you would for any business agreement, with full and specific detail. I was lucky enough to have Allison by my side to advise me at every stage and most of what you need to know is contained elsewhere in this book, but stick to your guns on this one – it's important!

Nearly two years and another house move later, involving a switch of county, we had secured a full Statement and 'Part 4' – the right school! We arrived at our new (rented) home penniless, exhausted and happy.

I still have to keep an eye on some of the provision he is actually receiving, mainly speech and language therapy, but with the Statement to refer to I can fairly quickly rectify any problems. The staff are truly wonderful, with real consideration and qualified help, and Jasper is now thriving. His grades are advancing all the time, and the main gallery in our town has exhibited three of his paintings. He has friends and his confidence has improved so much that he now rides to school on his scooter and is becoming the independent and talented young man that potentially he always was. He talks very clearly, using that lovely articulate vocabulary that he accumulated from reading old-fashioned Thomas the Tank Engine and factual books on transport. His handwriting has never been good because of his dyspraxia, but it is improving and he uses a computer like a professional. He says that when he goes to university he'd like to do that new film studies course we read about. Or maybe engineering.

All I have to do now is find a sixth form.

Jasper's side of the story

I can't remember much about being little; I remember crying at night, I don't know why. I used to have meltdowns, my mum said, but I don't remember having any. I was only little then and you can't expect people to remember everything. Our first house was huge, with a big garden, one time I got a bouncy castle for my birthday. I did like it there; it was a shame we had to move. I would like to live in a house like that again.

Classes in the nursery were named after Winnie the Pooh characters. Unfortunately every time you went up to the Tigger room with the older children there they dragged you back down, which was very annoying. That's where we met Jo, she came to play at our house, and I rather enjoyed her coming over. She used to tell stories about our crazy dog 'Tiger' the wonder dog.

We moved to another house. It was a lot smaller, it was ok and I had a friend who used to come and play. I don't often have friends to play. When I went to school it wasn't very nice there. I had to sit on a red mat, I wasn't very happy there. There were too many children and it was annoying. Some of the teachers were nice.

Home schooling was my favourite, I enjoyed it. I spent more time with mum and got to do stuff I don't usually do at school. Do more of my own thing. We made cakes, maps and loads of other things, I really did like it then.

Then I went to another school. It was for home schoolers like me. I liked it there. I made a large model of a train that I tried to fit myself into.

We moved again and mum managed to get the 00 scale model layout for me from the local steam railway. I really did like it. I had some friends in to play but they managed to damage a bit of the layout so I didn't want them to touch it again. The house was in a cul-de-sac, which according to Harry Hill is a good place for aliens as they have a round bit at the end to land their UFO on.

Then another school which was quite bad, one of the children threw one of my toys on the roof so that I couldn't get it. Another day he climbed on the roof himself, if you ask me he was mad! I remember one of the teachers was nice. She brought in her nice grey rabbit one day. We watched *Watership Down* (it was the 1990s version, not the 1970s version). To continue what I was saying, school was very hard. I kept being bullied there so out of there we went, in fact out of the town. They had a model train shop which was good; however, the appearance of the building was not good.

I went on some trials at some other schools. At one they had a mechanics workshop. They had a 1950s Morris Minor it was rather interesting. That version had the headlights in the grill instead of the usual position above the grill indicating that it was an early model. There was also a Jaguar XJ6, I can't remember the other cars. The school was rather ok. But it didn't go well; they were terrible when I got upset and they didn't know what to do. Eventually mum came and picked me up. I liked the cars, and the Tom and Jerry magazines.

We tried some other schools but they didn't work out well so we left.

We had to move house quite a lot of course, nearly all the time! It was a bit hard, you know. Especially when there was nothing in the house or the furniture was out of line and you didn't know where your things were.

I think mum and I found it very hard, especially when I couldn't find something I wanted to use.

Mum found my new school and we decided to go there and it was fine. I enjoy it there, they know what to do. I have made some friends, it is possibly the best school there is. It makes the other schools look terrible. I think the other ones were cheapskates if you ask me, they didn't want to buy the right equipment. I never want to go back to any of those other ones again. I like it where we live now; I'd possibly like to stay living here. I do like it here, you know. They have some rather interesting stuff.

I'm interested in trains, apparently Thomas the Tank Engine was the reason I got interested when I was little. I like to make movies, with my mum's camera, I have been making some funny films based on the movie *Cars* using the characters I have.

I don't really know what I'll do when I leave school; I'd like to stay on a bit longer until I make my mind up. Mum is trying to persuade the council to make a new school for some children when they are 16 so they can study more. I think it's a very good idea. I'll be supporting mum as I think it's a very good idea. I'm not sure what I'll do after I leave school. I'm hoping it will be rather good. It would be rather good you know.

Chapter 2

Your Special Child

Much of the literature available surrounding children with autism explains the disorder in terms of the 'triad of impairments'. What that means is that the definitions given are all about what a child will struggle with. Whilst this may be useful to underpin the development of programmes and a curriculum, it can be depressing and daunting to hear about all of the areas in which your child may have weaknesses. It is therefore vitally important that we look at each child on an individual basis and take into account his strengths, motivators, his personality and what makes him happy.

The following is a comment from a mother:

> As a parent one of the worst, but ultimately necessary activities (as part of the assessment procedure) in order to make qualified and supportive education available is the unpicking of your child's character. It can leave you feeling traumatised, deflated and questioning your child's obvious talents and abilities. This is very common – but try to understand that this is unfortunately part of the process and don't lose heart. They will always be the unique individual that you know and love; if this allows them to reach their potential then so be it.
>
> (Evelyn Ashford, 2010)

Many schools will work on the basis that children need to be given tasks which address their weaknesses and almost 'plug the gaps'. This is further exacerbated when documents such as education and behaviour support plans are produced which do not clearly state the talents that all of these young people have. Many children display a spiky profile which means that they may be extremely good in one subject area and not so good in another. There may be extreme variables with a subject area against NC scores, and forward-thinking schools are now using a 'best fit' approach to scoring pupils with autism. There is finally an understanding that not every single skill needs to be mastered before the child can move on to the next level. Furthermore, there is often a misconception that children with autism have a poor attention span. Again this is not true. Have a look at how long their attention span is when engaging in self-chosen activity. This is where they may really excel in the future. Many famous current and historical figures have been shown to have autism as a driving force behind their achievements, and employers should begin to see the benefits of employing people who are this focused.

It is vital that we allow for opportunities throughout the day for young people to experience success in engagement with activities which they are good at, and that they are not simply fed a diet of one task after another which they will struggle with. If you think of the subject that you hated most at school and try to imagine being forced to do this all day until you mastered it I am sure that your reaction to school and learning would not be good. Learning and programmes should be based on the five *Every Child Matters* outcomes which are: be healthy, stay safe, enjoy and achieve, make a positive contribution and achieve economic well-being.

Another major issue which can often be overlooked is the child's personality. Often children can be categorised by their disability rather than their wants and needs, and this would lead us to believe that all young people with ASD will present in the same way. We all know this not to be true.

Some young people with ASD have experienced very difficult times in educational establishments which, however well meaning, have not met their needs. Some children will have missed out on years of appropriate education but are still expected to cope with transition at the age of 16. In these instances it is important that this is recognised and that expectations and demands are altered accordingly. On entry to a new school it may be that the young person is only given tasks that he can succeed with so that he has a sense of achievement from day one. It may be that this will lead to working with emerging skills.

The use of 'errorless learning', a technique developed by Terrance (1963) which limits the number of errors that can be made by reducing the opportunity for incorrect choice, can also be a useful technique to give young people instant success. Another technique which has been shown to be successful is chaining. This can be either backwards or forwards and essentially breaks down a task into its component parts. So, for example, making a cup of tea would be broken down into selecting the cup, selecting a teabag, placing the teabag in the cup and so on. Each component part is taught by modelling to the child. In forward chaining the child is taught the first part of the task and the following component parts are undertaken by the instructor. In backward chaining the instructor will undertake the initial component parts of a task and the child will undertake the final part to complete. This again is a technique which can give the capacity for success. It is extremely important to make sure that every day has a moment which is good, however difficult the day has been, and that every day starts afresh.

Motivation is key in wanting to achieve and this should be built into any programme or activity. This, if at all possible, should be naturally occurring motivation and may be linked to special interests. I had the pleasure of working with a young boy who had an obsessional interest in videos. To work with this interest, part of his learning was delivered through video. He was able, through this medium, to re-wind and re-visit vocabulary that he needed further exposure to. Within six months he learned to speak French at such a level that he was able to help his parents on a family holiday to France. Obviously this method may not work for all and not all learning will be motivational. To compensate for this, small, less desirable tasks can be followed by activities which are really enjoyed. A good way of celebrating success in mastering a task is to generalise it. This can involve giving opportunities to practise the skill in a non threatening environment, and learning ways in which the skill can be applied and then being supported to use this skill.

Two other issues which may hinder performance are useful to know about. The first is a condition known as hyperlexia, which is the ability to read without understanding the content of what has been read. It can be hugely frustrating for a child to be offered comprehension tasks against a text that he does not understand. The second is dysgraphia, which is a condition where a person finds it difficult to write. This presents as poor motor coordination and a lack of organisation and presentation of written material. Writing usually lacks sequence, spelling and punctuation may be poor and letters may be inappropriately sized or spaced. If a child is presenting with dysgraphia then there will be a need to improve his handwriting skills and possibly to provide an alternative to writing, such as the use of a laptop.

Young people with autism are able to teach us different ways of viewing the world, and many have huge strengths in areas that non autistic people, and particularly young people, often find difficult. They tend to be very good at analysing and remembering detail, as well as being very logical and literal in their interpretation and perception. Their rote memory can be very good and they are often very dependable and honest. Some people with autism have the ability to mono focus and complete tasks without distraction as well as superior sensory acumen. Other traits which are often present include extreme productivity, self-teaching and the ability to follow rules, policy and procedure to the letter.

Some young people with autism have very special skills and are known as 'autistic savants'. Happé and Frith (2009) unpick the basis of this phenomenon in their paper 'The beautiful otherness of the autistic mind', which is well worth a read. There are also many other accounts of young people who display incredible feats of memory and recall, as well as exceptional skills in the areas of art, music and maths, to name but a few. There have been many famous savants, and I will mention a few who have been significantly prolific to raise the awareness of this fascinating condition.

- Ros Blackburn is a woman in her 40s who was considered to be profoundly affected by her autism as a child. She is now able to talk about her experiences and her perception of the world. She is said to have savant abilities in her use of language, which she calls her 'freak peak', and her insight has had a significant effect on the way that professionals view children with autism.

- Many marvel at the work of Stephen Wiltshire, an autistic savant who is able to view extremely complex structures for just a few moments and then draw them with absolute accuracy with no further reference. His work is now world famous and much has been documented around this incredible skill.

- Daniel Tammet, the author of *Born on a Blue Day*, can undertake the most complex of mathematical calculations in a fraction of the time that others using a calculator are able to achieve. His book is a fascinating account of how he perceives the world.

- Tito Mukhopadhyay is an author, poet and philosopher who lives in India. He has a remarkable ability to use language in his work even though he is severely autistic.

- The film *Rain Man* was one of the first mainstream films to portray a person with autism who also had savant skills in the ability to recall and card count. This character was based upon the real-life person Kim Peek who was understood to have autism at the time and presented in a way which suggested that he was a savant. This diagnosis, however, has recently been changed.

It is believed that about 10 per cent of all people with autism have special skills. They may range from obsessive remembering and retrieval of facts on areas of interest to the ability to undertake a task such as playing a complex piece of music on a piano with no training after hearing it just once.

I have worked with many young people who display islets of ability ranging from those who can recall the order of a pack of shuffled cards after viewing them just once to those who complete 500-piece jigsaws face down in less than a minute. Some surprise you with their ability to understand, such as an 11-year-old girl with severe autism who threw away her social story that staff had written for her and rewrote it in a much more effective manner! Some children will astound with their sheer determination to get things right and keep on going.

It must be extremely difficult to exist in a heightened state of anxiety for most of the time, trying to make sense of a world that is nonsensical and to understand people who often speak a different language from you. It is to be applauded that these people continue to make progress in their lives despite the hurdles that are put in their way. This has to be something to celebrate.

Chapter 3

Diagnosis of an Autistm Spectrum Disorder

It is likely that you have had concerns for some time about how your child is behaving and performing to suspect that he may have autism, AS or a communication difficulty. Some parents talk of knowing almost from birth, whilst some state that they knew that their child was 'different' but could not really explain why. There is a strong genetic component in autism and it may be that you have other members of the family with the condition which has allowed you to make some comparisons. Whatever the reasons, it is useful to investigate fully your concerns and then decide if you wish to pursue a formal assessment to gain a clearer picture of your child and confirm whether or not he has autism.

Many families adjust to the demands of an autistic child almost without realising that they have done so. They provide compensatory environments which can minimise the basis of anxiety and alleviate some of the stress their child experiences, particularly in social situations, and so reduce behaviours which challenge the child and others. Parents can then be very distressed when their child enters an environment that is not knowledgeable and sensitive to their needs and does not accommodate and adjust to these needs, particularly if it is a school. Many parents talk of the difficulties in taking their child into community facilities or to shops where there is high social demand and expectation and sensory overload. Families learn to find the parts of their community where the child feels comfortable and secure and can avoid others.

Community access can be the source of much distress to a young person with autism. Many experience sensory overload and struggle to understand the world around them. This can lead to inappropriate and potentially dangerous behaviours such as screaming, hitting, running off and engaging with people and objects in an unusual way. With an understanding of why these behaviours occur, young people with autism can be taught skills to manage difficult situations and to show others how to help them.

Schools can be difficult places for young people with autism to access, and without adjustment to meet their particular needs this can lead to problems. Some schools have a good understanding of the impact of educating children with autism, and with few adjustments your child may thrive. Others, however, do not necessarily understand ASD and your child may be seen as – and labelled as – uncooperative, avoidant, naughty or even aggressive. For these reasons it is important to share your child's autism with teachers and others in order to gain the support he needs. You know your child best, so do not be afraid to share approaches and strategies that you have found to be successful. It is vital that you are open and honest about your child, as it may be very damaging for him to be misunderstood.

The benefits of early diagnosis and intervention have been the source of much research and discussion by professionals involved in the field. There is currently an inconsistent approach to assessment and it will vary depending on where you live. However, a developmental assessment should indicate if your child requires further investigation. In the first instance it is likely that the recommendation will be for a general developmental assessment (GDA) to be undertaken. The National Autism Plan for Children (NAPC) guidance (NIASA 2003) suggests that waiting for a routine check should be avoided and concerns should be raised with a professional such as a health visitor, teacher or general practitioner (GP) as soon as possible so that these can be fully discussed and appropriate action taken.

When outlining these concerns be as explicit as possible. It may be a good idea to write down the reasons you think your child may have a problem or an ASD. Look at the diagnostic criteria and try to write down examples which illustrate some of these. It can be useful at this stage to contact the NAS for their publication list then go to your local library and read as much as you can. There is a wealth of information on the internet; try to be as informed as you can.

If it is agreed that a GDA is necessary, a paediatrician will talk to you about your child's developmental history. This may be at your local hospital or at a specific assessment centre. This should lead to a decision about the likelihood of the presence of an ASD. This is undertaken by the NHS and should not cost you anything.

You can pay privately for an opinion from an independent educational psychologist, a consultant at a private assessment centre or, usually via a referral from your GP, a consultant paediatrician. This can be extremely costly but can cut down on waiting times. Alternatively, it may be necessary if professionals you have seen locally do not agree with your opinion on the nature and type of the problem.

If the GDA indicates the likelihood of an ASD a further multi-agency assessment will be undertaken which involves a team of different types of professional (e.g. speech and language therapist; teacher; psychologist; occupational therapist) and this may lead to a diagnosis. It is unlikely that you will receive a diagnosis immediately as observations and reports may be required from a number of settings. For some children further assessments may also be undertaken to rule out the possibility of other medical conditions. You should receive a written report which will include a summary of the child's needs and recommendations of how he should be supported. This report may include a diagnosis. At this stage you may also receive information about local services and support networks, as well as LA provision and SEN procedures. It may be worth contacting your local Parent Partnership Services (PPS) as it will be able to provide information on SEN provision. Its advice is neutral and may help you to identify and make sense of the support available.

A document outlining the coordination and support should be given as well as a date for ongoing reviews of the situation. The NAPC (NIASA 2003) provides a pro forma of the assessment tools used and has a useful flowchart with suggested timeframes for this process.

For children over five years old, referral may be made to your local Child and Adolescent Mental Health Services (CAMHS). This should lead to a multi-disciplinary developmental diagnostic assessment, which in turn should provide the information required for diagnosis. Your GP should be able to advise you as to the likely route for assessment. Some children may have more obvious difficulties than others and so make the diagnosis easier. The SEN Code of Practice (DfES 2001) sets out requirements for assessment, and schools are expected to assess and address SEN as they arise, as well as keeping the LA and parents informed.

Many young people with autism are not diagnosed until they are of school age and beyond. This may be particularly true of those with AS or HFA. Without a diagnosis, their behaviours can be misinterpreted and misunderstood and sanctions applied, rather than support given. This can then lead to depression in the child, as he knows that he is in some way different but has no tangible explanation. It is not always appropriate or necessary for a young person to have a formal diagnosis if he is not experiencing any problems which affect his emotional well-being and progress. The lack of a diagnosis can, however, in some instances lead to restricted access to services. Whether or not to seek a diagnosis should be fully discussed with all parties involved and the implications of this examined. Murray (2006) has compiled a very useful book which explores the benefits and potential disadvantages of having a diagnosis and sharing it with others.

Your child's school can help. You can request that an educational psychologist observe your child in school. This can lead to a recommendation of an educational assessment, as well as a detailed identification of need and support required. Further information on requesting a Statutory Assessment which may lead to a Statement of SEN from the LA is detailed in Chapter 10. The NAS will have details of support groups in your area which many parents find very helpful. Contact a Family (CaF) also has details of all national support groups.

The early recognition of an ASD is important, and if you firmly believe that your child may have autism do not rest until your child has been assessed.

Many individuals who have autism remain undiagnosed for their whole lives. Indeed, the condition was only recognised less than 70 years ago by Leo Kanner (1943) and Hans Asperger (1944). I don't particularly hold with the notion that it is better not to be labelled, as securing a diagnosis may give access to support and help. It will also explain to the child why he is different from other children and will give opportunities to develop strategies to manage these differences where necessary. However, as a parent it is a choice that you will have to make. You may decide to seek a diagnosis and not share this with your child. I have supported many families who have made this choice and who feel that it was right for them. I have also supported children who are confused and sad that they cannot make sense of why they are different from their peers. It is a decision that you will have to think about and discuss with significant others before settling on your course of action.

I am sure that we all know of people, including ourselves, who are bound by routines and order. To state that this is a bit autistic is to make the analogy that you can be a little psychopathic because you don't feel empathy for certain people and situations. To get a diagnosis of autism, a person has to display features in all three key areas, not just in one. There is nothing that a child with autism does that typical children and adults do not do at some time, so it is not sensible to label a person as autistic just because he engages in behaviours that are seen in autism. Autism has been described as an extreme form of maleness as men tend to display more behaviours seen in autism than women. As autism 'shades into normality', there is a question as to how many behaviours must be displayed, or how seriously different a child or adult has to be to qualify for a diagnosis. The key question to ask is whether a child or adult would benefit in any way from having the diagnosis of an ASD. If it would help the child or the school or the family to understand and support the child, then having a diagnosis would be of use. But if the child or adult is only mildly different (slightly unusual in his behaviour or interests), then it may not be that helpful and may work against his best interests. Some children and adults who have been given the diagnosis have been very upset by it, sometimes because of the negative literature which exists, but the majority of adults with an ASD have said that knowing their diagnosis has helped them to understand themselves and to develop their own strategies to cope in a world which seems alien. It may be that your health visitor has expressed concerns over the development of your child, or that as a parent you have a suspicion that something may be not quite right. It is important to be clear as to why you have concerns and to make a list prior to discussing this with professionals.

Children with an ASD will display impairments in social understanding and interaction and in communication, as well as restricted and repetitive patterns of behaviour. A number of checklists are used for screening, prior to using a diagnostic assessment procedure. Some of these screening tools are general developmental checklists such as Ages and Stages (Squires *et al.* 2009) and Parents' Evaluation of Developmental Status (PEDS) (Glascoe, Maclean and Stone 1991), and some are autism-specific such as the Autism Observation Scale for Infants (AOSI) (Bryson *et al.* 2008), the Social Communication Questionnaire (SCQ) (Wing *et al.* 2002) and the Modified Checklist for Autism in Toddlers (M-CHAT) (Baron-Cohen *et al.* 2000). Most of these can be downloaded from the internet. These will flag up any concern in an area of development and then other diagnostic instruments can be used to provide more detail. Children can be screened as early as 12 months; however, undertaking this process too early may give a misleading result as the rate at which children develop in the early months can vary considerably.

Most screening takes place between 24 and 36 months. In 2007 the American Academy of Pediatrics identified some 'Red Flags' which may indicate the presence of an ASD and can be used from as early as 12 months (American Academy of Pediatrics 2007). The full range can be found on the internet but include the following: no babbling or pointing or other gesture by 12 months; no single words by 16 months; no two-word spontaneous phrases by 24 months; and loss of language or social skills at any age.

Instruments used to diagnose autism are varied and include the Childhood Autism Rating Scale (CARS) (Schopler, Reichler and Renner 1988), the Diagnostic Interview for Social and Communication Disorders (DISCO) (Leekam *et al.* 2002), the Autism Diagnostic Interview (ADI) (Le Couteur, Lord and Rutter 2003) and the Autism Diagnostic Observation Schedule (ADOS) (Lord *et al.* 2002). These consist of taking information from interviews with parents, a medical history and observation.

There are two main international systems used for the diagnosis of autism:

1. The ICD-10 (International Classification of Diseases) diagnostic criteria for childhood autism and AS (WHO 1993)

   The full list of criteria can be found by following the link: www.who.int/classifications/icd/en/GRNBOOK.pdf

   Childhood autism (search for F84.0)

   Asperger's syndrome (F84.5)

2. The DSM-IV (Diagnostic and Statistical Manual) diagnostic categories for autistic disorder and Asperger's Disorder (American Psychiatric Association 1994)

   The full criteria can be found by following the link: www.autism-pdd.net/checklist.html (click on diagnostic criteria).

   Autistic Disorder (299.00)

   Asperger's Disorder (299.80)

   This scale is currently being revised and it is likely that the terms autism, Asperger Syndrome and Pervasive Developmental Disorder (not otherwise specified) (PDD (NOS)) will all fall under the heading of ASD. This poses some interesting questions for access to services for young people with AS.

Autism is not a disease or illness but a result of neurological and developmental differences. The most effective ways to help children and adults with an ASD are both educational and psychological as these help the individual to develop strategies to understand how to communicate, how to operate in social situations and how to understand himself. With appropriate interventions and programmes many young people with autism are able to lead very positive and successful lives and develop skills necessary for independence. A review of the evidence on the effectiveness of interventions by Jordan, Jones and Murray (1998) suggested that early intervention and structure, routine and predictability were key to supporting these young people most effectively to allow them to reach their potential.

Medication

The use of medication to treat the symptoms of autism has been a vigorously debated topic for many years. Often parents and schools have opposing views, and this can cause an erosion of relationships and trust. If a few simple guidelines are adhered to a more informed decision can be made.

- Medication for behaviour management should not be the first intervention.

- Medication may form part of a proactive programme which includes behavioural support and educational programmes.

- Medication should not be used as a 'chemical cosh' for children who have challenging behaviours.

- Any medical intervention should be thoroughly explored in terms of long-term risk versus short-term gains.

- Any medical intervention needs to be closely monitored and evaluated on a regular basis.

- All side effects of medication should be fully explored prior to administration.

If a child had a chest infection we would seek out medication to aid his recovery. If a child has epilepsy we tend to be fairly comfortable about administering medication on a long-term basis. We do, however, tend to be less comfortable about using medication to reduce anxiety in children with autism. It is true that some medication can pose long-term health risks, but this needs to be weighed up against the potential benefits. If a child with autism can access learning more effectively by reducing his anxiety with medication the long-term benefits could be huge. There is no right or wrong answer in the debate regarding medication; however, it may be something that you wish to discuss further with your doctor or other medical professional.

KEY POINTS

- Parents will need to examine and discuss the implications of seeking out a diagnosis.

- Lack of diagnosis can lead to prohibited access to support services.

- In the first instance it is likely that a GDA will be undertaken.

- Routes to diagnosis can be via your GP, school or CAMHS team, or through private independent assessment.

- Some people do not receive a diagnosis until they are of school age and beyond.

- Some parents will seek out a diagnosis and this may help with access to services; others do not want their child labelled and so will not want a formal diagnosis.

- The two main international systems for diagnosing autism are the ICD-10 and the DCM-IV; however, there are various other diagnostic instruments and screening tools.

- The appropriate programme and interventions can make an enormous difference to progress and well-being.

- The use of medication should be well monitored and should usually form part of a wider package of intervention.

Chapter 4

$\sim\!\!\sim\!\!\sim\!\!\sim$

Practical Strategies to Support your Child with Autism

Young people with autism can struggle to make sense of the world and this can lead to inappropriate or challenging behaviours. If we can begin to understand the function of behaviours, that is, why a person is responding in a certain way, then we may be able to provide more effective strategies for him to develop more appropriate or socially acceptable behaviours. If we can understand the basis of why a child responds in a certain manner, then we can teach new skills which achieve the same outcome or have the same function.

The triad of impairments is a deficit model and does not acknowledge the unique skills that a child with autism has. However, it can be a useful tool to provide an overview of why he may struggle to understand or manage certain situations or concepts.

Communication and language

Difficulties in understanding the language of others (receptive language) can lead to children with ASD appearing to be stubborn and non compliant. Sometimes they do not make eye contact with others and this can be misconstrued as not listening or attending. These young people may also experience problems reading non verbal gestures and so will not notice when people are becoming angry or upset. These are not deliberate responses and are certainly not designed to irritate, but they can be interpreted as such by those who do not know about autism.

It can be useful to use the child's name at the beginning of communication so that he knows that you are talking to him, and to keep language simple and non ambiguous. When giving instructions, try to adjust to the level of your child's understanding. It may be that the child is only able to hold one instruction in his head at a time, and so complex instructions such as 'Take your coat off, sit down and eat your sandwich' will lead to the child taking his coat off and then wondering what is meant to happen next.

Some young people process language very slowly and need additional time to understand what has been said. You should allow up to ten seconds for this processing to occur. There is a danger, if you do not get a response from the child straight away, that you repeat what you have asked. You can imagine how confusing it may be for a child to be halfway through processing an instruction and then for the adult to offer more language to process at the same time. It can be helpful to remember to wait for a few moments after giving an instruction and then if you need to repeat the instruction to use the same words in the same order so as not to confuse.

The use of visual cues can also be a great support in the development of language and communication skills. Children with autism struggle with abstract concepts, preferring the literal and concrete. Schedules or timetables can be a great aid at home to help with predicting what will happen and in what order. They can also be useful in developing a child's understanding of the passage of time, and how long he will have to wait before a favoured activity will happen.

Some children with autism will struggle with recalling events that have happened to them (e.g. when the teacher asks them to share their news) although they may have a good rote memory. This can be exacerbated by the fact that they often struggle to tell others the gist of an event and instead give lots of detailed descriptions which are not necessary to the story.

Many young people with autism find it very hard to make a choice between multiple items. In the first instance it may help to give a closed choice (e.g. this or that) before progressing to a greater number of options. Choice boards with photographs of options can also help some young people with this concept.

Sentence construction may be skewed and often children with an ASD will refer to themselves by name rather than 'I' or 'me' (e.g.

'Ben wants a biscuit', instead of 'I want a biscuit'). Some children will display echolalic speech, which is the repetition of something that they have heard previously, with little understanding of its meaning or use. It is thought by some that this repetition of what they have heard helps them to process the meaning. It is important to realise from this that people might then assume that the child has higher-level language skills than is actually the case.

Children and adults with autism have huge problems in understanding what to do and say, and when. Our social behaviour changes with the social context (e.g. home; school; work; church; library; theatre). Teaching children with autism all the different rules is extremely difficult. They need to be taught these in the real situation as far as possible so that they make the link with what is expected and where. They will need to be given advice on making eye contact, listening, turn-taking, how close to stand to another person, and the tone of voice, volume and rate of speaking, for example. There is a wealth of literature available on this topic which may help to support your child's development. The NAS produces book lists which may help.

If a child does not understand what is being asked of him, or cannot communicate his needs, this is likely to lead to frustration and anxiety. It is vital that we give children the skills to communicate their needs as effectively as possible.

Social understanding and relationships

Almost all young people with autism will struggle with social interaction and understanding. A common trait is for children to state something they think without being aware of the social implications such as, 'You have had your hair cut and I don't think that it suits you', or, 'You're no good at football'. Sometimes the issues faced by young people with AS can be masked by seemingly good language skills. They will be able to use language in a formal way, but may struggle with understanding how to join a conversation, appropriate topics and modifying what they are saying and how they are talking to the listener. They can also use over-formal greetings, struggling to understand how to change their language to fit the age, status and sex of their audience, for example.

It is important that you create opportunities for your child to interact with others in a non threatening and safe way. It is also important not to force him to be social as this is often the area of life children with autism find most difficult and exposing them to parties or family gatherings can be highly anxiety-provoking and stressful. It is important to help your child to tolerate the company of other children and adults, but this should be done in a planned and staged way so that he learns to understand the potential benefits, rather than having his view confirmed that being social is awful. To be successful it is likely that the child will need some support in the understanding of the rules of social engagement. It can be useful to try to develop an interest that can be shared with others, such as construction or model making, or to find a group which shares the child's special interest (e.g. in dinosaurs or a TV programme or character).

Thinking and behaving in a flexible way

It is common for children with ASD to focus on the details of an event or situation and to take longer to grasp the meaning of the whole (often referred to as weak central coherence). This can affect their ability to generalise objects into categories and thus have an understanding that, for example, although not all chairs look the same they are all chairs and they all perform the same function. Some young people with autism overgeneralise, such as believing that all animals with four legs are dogs. It can be of great help to point out which features can aid in this categorisation. When teaching how to make a cup of tea, for example, it will be important that you use a range of different cups, teabags from different boxes and milk from different containers as this generalisation of items does not always naturally occur. Functionality of objects can also be an issue with young people, who may know the name of an object but have very little idea about its use.

Changes to routine can cause major anxiety and distress. This may be due to poor executive functioning, whereby planning and predicting skills are poor. Many young people with autism find, for example, that if they get stuck halfway through a task, such as making a sandwich and finding out that there is no peanut butter, they are unable to change tack and make the sandwich with a different filling.

Teaching these skills will be most effective in real-life situations, and setting up realistic challenges so that they have to problem-solve is very helpful. It is also worth thinking about teaching a social skill for life, as once a skill is taught it will take a lot of undoing. A common one which springs to mind is holding other people's hands. Whilst this is perfectly acceptable behaviour between a mother and her five year old, it becomes less acceptable for an 18-year-old adult and his carer. Linking arms may be a good alternative which would keep the young child safe but is also a skill which is fitting for an older person.

One of the features of autism can be an all-encompassing interest and this can lead to a child engaging with a particular activity, book or DVD for hours on end. Often this is coupled with talking about the interest to anyone who will listen without the realisation that it is boring for the listener. Children with autism often expect the listener to be equally interested in the topic. Special interests can be built upon and used to make a deal with the child, so that when he does a task which is less desirable, he is rewarded with time on his special interest. Special interests can also lead to careers or enjoyable leisure activities.

Sensory issues

Many young people with autism have problems knowing where their body is in space and with balance. They may be clumsy as a result and bump into people and furniture, or seek out opportunities to feel their bodies more definitely by engaging in activities such as spinning, rocking or lying across the table or on the floor. Although not part of the triad of impairments, it is a widely held belief that most young people with autism have significant sensory issues. Many find it a challenge to process sensory information effectively (e.g. when two people talk at once; screening out irrelevant sounds or sights in and outside of the classroom and focusing only on the most relevant). What this actually means is that too much information is perceived by one or more of the senses and this can lead to sensory overload. An example of this would be a child walking into a restaurant. The walls are covered in pictures, the counters are covered in food and a number of people are chatting. The child may find that instead of getting the 'gist' that it must be a café or a restaurant, he becomes totally overwhelmed by the amount of sensory information received and tries to manage this by focusing on the detail of one thing, such as the light switch or the number of cheese sandwiches. It is a way of coping and shutting out much of the other sensory information.

People process information through their senses and most are able to integrate the material to make it meaningful. Returning again to the scenario of walking into a restaurant, the visual information received would translate into an understanding that food could be bought and consumed in this room and therefore this building is likely to be a café or restaurant. It would not be necessary to look individually at each food product available; rather a brief look would confirm that a range of food products was available. The smell of the room would confirm that food was in fact being prepared, and the noise of food being cooked and consumed would further direct understanding. The other two senses of taste and touch could also be used to make an informed guess as to the function of the room. Young people with ASD can struggle to combine these pieces of information to reach a reasonable conclusion.

It is interesting to note that many schools make considerable use of supermarkets and shopping when teaching life skills. These shops are some of the most sensory-laden environments ever encountered. Visually they are incredibly busy, with different shapes of packaging and point-of-sale material as well as fluorescent lights which can be a big problem for people with autism. In fact, it is often in this setting that we hear anecdotal tales of the scenes caused when a child with undiagnosed autism experiences this environment, including the disapproving glances from other shoppers!

Supermarkets often have strong smells which change as you walk around, and the temperature can change too. The array of noises can be vast with the scanning at the tills, chatter, the noise of shopping trolleys and often piped music and tannoy announcements. It may be better as a start to use a small, lower-arousal shop and to work up to larger establishments when the child has more experience and understanding.

Many young people with autism struggle to moderate sensory processing and this can take the form of having heightened responses to smell, only tolerating a limited range of food and disliking touch (especially light touch). It is important that we are aware of the impact that sensory issues can have and to be aware that poor sensory integration can lead to a person with autism seeking out self-stimulatory behaviours to block out this overload. This can take the form of flicking, rocking, flapping or making noises. It can be useful, if a person does not respond well to loud or unexpected noise, to use headphones or an mp3 player to reduce the impact of this. It is also common for people with autism to under-respond to pain and so not report illness or injury, which can obviously have very serious consequences.

Repetitive and rigid behaviours

Many young people with autism will display stereotypical behaviours. These are repetitive movements of parts of or the whole of the body. This can involve hand flapping, arm waving, clapping, rocking and spinning. Some young people walk on their toes and some engage in whole body movements. Some young people find these movements calming and will engage in them when happy or when absorbed in topics of particular interest.

Some young people with autism perform complex ritualistic behaviours not unlike those associated with obsessive compulsive disorder (OCD). These can involve crossing a threshold, such as a door, a number of times. Children can get locked into these repetitive patterns of behaviour and it may be that a clinical psychologist is needed to develop a programme to support the young person and reduce the behaviour. Obsessively lining up items and making collections of objects can also be signs of inner anxiety which may require to be addressed with more specialist advice.

Anxiety remains at the heart of autism, and the issues which have been explored above can leave a young person on the edge of coping most of the time. In this emotional state it might take very little to go from 'just coping' to 'not coping' and this can often be the trigger for challenging or socially inappropriate behaviours to occur.

There are many approaches which may help your child and in the following pages a few ways of working are outlined that you may find useful. I have also included the rationale behind these so that you can modify your response if need be, while still understanding the basis for the approach. I have given some real-life examples to illustrate.

Attending

- Always start any communication by saying the child's name.

- If looking at or attending to things is an issue, then use a torch in a darkened room to get the child to follow the light with his gaze and then look at an object together.

- Use concrete props to support attending, such as items that are mentioned in a story.

- Use sand timers or kitchen timers so that the child knows how long he will be expected to engage in an activity.

A child whose attending skills were extremely limited had a special interest in Pingu. Cards were made with pictures on them attached to a string 'washing line' which depicted parts of the story. He was able to run his hands down the string and stop and look at the picture as the story was read to him. The pictures were then used to sequence the story, which also aided in the development of his attention skills.

Coping with new things

- Use pictures and video to introduce a new situation, setting or activity.

- Use a social story.

- Allow your child to explore in whichever way he wishes (e.g. mouthing or smelling objects).

- Allow your child time to process information.

A child who was terrified of the school minibus refused to go anywhere near it. He had not seen a minibus before and had no concept of its purpose. Pictures were taken of the outside and inside of the bus and a book made for the child. This also included pictures of the minibus at the child's favourite places. The child was encouraged to go and look at the outside of the bus and the inside from the door. Finally, a favoured object was placed inside the bus with a reward next to it. Once he had accessed the minibus he was no longer frightened.

Organisational skills

- Use timetables.

- Use charts.

- Use work schedules (e.g. sequence the order of tasks visually).

A child would get very distressed when getting dressed as he attempted to do this in the wrong sequence (e.g. putting his pants over his trousers). A sequence of pictures was made which showed the order to put his clothes on, going from left to right, and this was stuck on the wall. It was highly successful and the distress was removed.

Rigid thinking patterns

- Make explicit connections.

- Use cards to sequence more than one ending to a situation so that the child builds up a portfolio of possible outcomes.

- Give examples of 'what could happen next'.

A child was taken for the day to a new carer whom he had not met before. Short-term care had not previously been a good experience as he had been taken to an emergency unit when his mother was ill. He refused to get out of the car when he arrived and became very distressed. Eventually he was taken home again. Over a period of time staff talked to him about short-term care and made a visual book of what would happen. Finally, he confided that the reason that he did not want to go was that he did not know when he would be brought home. So staff created a calendar which showed clearly the days he was in the short-term care home and the days he would be at home. He was then able to go to the short term-care home with less anxiety.

Literal language

- Don't avoid using metaphors and jokes. Use these to teach alternative meanings.

A child had been bought a new shirt for school from the clothing retailer George. It was different from his previous shirt as it was a cotton shirt rather than the polo shirt that he was used to. He had requested the new shirt to be more like his brother. He came home very upset with his mother stating that she had bought the shirt from a second hand shop. His mother denied this and said that it was in fact new. He then turned to his mother and said, 'Well why does it say George on the label? That's not my name.'

Extracting meaning from text

- Pick out key words.

- Use visual and contextual clues to help make a guess about the gist of a story.

A story was read to a young girl about a fête held on the village green. It outlined how the main character had won the cake-making competition. However, it transpired that she had in fact bought the cake rather than making it by hand. When asked about the gist of the story the young girl thought that it may be about the ducks on the pond or the flowers on the front of the cottage. Copies of parts of the pictures in the book were made and this helped her to identify key words in the text. The pictures and words were then placed in order. With these prompts she was able to talk about the sequence of events and the main events. This gave her a pro forma to use in the future when exploring the meanings in other stories.

Pedantic, over-formal language

- Teach a number of greetings for different audiences.

- Offer suggestions of less formal language.

A young boy aged eight was encouraged to shake hands with his new head teacher when he joined the school. This was used alongside the very formal greeting, 'Good morning, sir'. He then used this greeting with everyone, including his peers. Groups of people were identified with whom he would come into contact and a scripted greeting was devised for each group. A visual representation was made to remind him of these.

Over-literal response to rules

- Offer examples where rules do not need to be adhered to.

- Check your child's understanding of language or rules.

Many years ago, before school rules were written in a positive manner, I undertook some work in a school where one of the rules was 'No hitting or kicking'. The children understood what this meant and behaved accordingly most of the time. However, one girl with autism was completely thrown by this. When we went outside to play tennis she flatly refused to join in, stating that it was against the rules and that she would be punished. I explained to her that the school rule was about children and not objects and so hitting a ball was fine. I also explained that sometimes rules could be overridden and we talked about some concrete examples of when this could happen. For example, there is a sign in the park saying that you must not walk on the grass but the park keeper is allowed because he has to cut the grass. We made up a book of rules that she was aware of and put examples of when certain rules could be broken or not fully adhered to.

Bullying

- Be clear about what constitutes bullying.

- Offer practical advice of how to avoid this.

- Give details of who the child can talk to if he is worried.

A very distressed child stated in circle time that he was being bullied by another student in the class. When asked what he meant by bullying he said that it was when someone else was not being nice. It transpired that the person who he believed was bullying him actually just wanted some time alone. A whole module of work was undertaken with the class which explored the notion of bullying so that everyone had a better understanding of how to define it and what it actually meant. Staff also introduced the child who thought that he was being bullied to other children who wanted to play reciprocal games.

Explosive responses

- Notice triggers to behaviour and try to distract your child.

- Divert attention to an activity your child enjoys.

- Reduce your language to a minimum when your child is anxious.

- Try to remove your child to a safe space.

- If your child is distressed, make the space safe, move away and stay at a distance from him and wait.

- Allow for recovery afterwards.

- Try to understand what caused the behaviour and teach your child more effective ways of managing this.

- Understand situations which may cause anxiety and teach tolerance or ways to avoid these.

A pupil loved to type lyrics by her favourite singer on the computer; however, after a time this pleasurable activity would take her to a state of arousal in which she would become very anxious and challenging. Staff were loath to remove this activity completely as it was a powerful motivator. She was given a sand timer to limit the amount of time that she was allowed to engage in this activity and to introduce the notion of safe space. Initially if she started to become anxious she would require a prompt to go and sit on her beanbag in a quiet room. A tactile ball was given for her to run through her hands. In time she was able to take herself off to her safe space without prompting and understood that her time on the computer had finished, using the sand timer as a reference.

Use of safe space

- Agree a place to which your child can remove himself if anxiety starts to build.

- A beanbag can be useful for your child to sit on in his safe space. Make sure that he does not see this as a punishment.

- Make sure that the area in the safe space is low arousal.

- Leave your child to calm down using minimal language.
- Some children like calming music but others do not.
- Provide a drink when your child is calm.

A number of children run away when they are anxious and the introduction of a safe space gives them the opportunity to move physically, which shifts activity from thinking to doing. Most are happy to run to a pre-agreed safe space.

Emotional understanding

- Teach your child to recognise the physical feelings linked to basic emotions.
- Teach your child about his own emotions first.
- Use visual cues of expressions to teach children about their own emotions and those of others.
- Teach rules around this. For example, if someone is crying it is likely that he is upset.

A pupil in a mainstream school experienced problems reading the emotions of others, and this would lead him into very difficult situations. One of the things that he was unable to spot was when others around him were starting to display anger. He had been caught in the middle of fights on a number of occasions as he would not notice that people were getting angry and confrontational until it was too late. Staff worked with him using role-play and taught him about the outward signs of anger, particularly the early stages, without putting him at risk.

Fact and fiction

- Teach your child to tell the difference between pretend and real.
- Teach using the benchmark 'Is this likely to be real?'

A child in a special school was teased because he believed that Super Ted was real. If anyone said that he was not, the pupil would go into a rage, shouting that of course Super Ted was real. Staff discussed a number of fictional characters with him, examining the question, 'Is this character likely to be real?' There was also discussion around how many teddy bears he had seen that were able to talk and fly. Staff explained that fictional characters were good fun and did not have to be real to be important. A scripted response was developed that he could use with his peers whereby he stated, 'I know that Super Ted is not real but I still like to watch him on TV.' The teasing very soon stopped and the pupil had new points of reference to make more effective judgements about fact and fiction.

Stranger danger

- Give clear definitions of who a stranger is and who could be a friend.

- Give examples of how to check out what you think.

- Give a scripted response such as, 'I cannot stay here with you because you are a stranger.'

It is vitally important that stranger danger is taught to all young people, but for those with autism it becomes even more important because they can be extremely vulnerable. One student went off with someone he did not know who happened to have a dog. When later questioned, the child stated that the person was not a stranger as they knew the dog. These assumptions about how to define a stranger were discussed and challenged to increase this child's awareness.

Use of pronouns

- Model how to use 'I' and 'me'.

- Explain that your child is an 'I' and a 'me'.

- Use visual cueing, for example touching your chest when saying 'I' or 'me' and prompting the child to do the same.

A pupil who could not understand and did not use pronouns was always referring to herself by name. An aide memoire was placed in front of her desk which said '***** is an I, ***** is a me. Come and get a reward when you say "I" and "me".' The reward had been agreed with the pupil, and this was a very successful way to introduce this vocabulary to her.

Deception

- Children with autism are unlikely to be able to understand or engage in telling lies as they struggle to understand the intentions of others.

- Children with autism can, however, understand deception on a concrete level.

I do hope that the examples given have been useful and that they give some ideas about how best to address some of the issues. Make sure that you work with outside agencies to develop consistent practices that help to develop lifelong learning skills in a range of settings.

KEY POINTS

- It is important that we understand the function of inappropriate behaviour to allow effective modification to occur.

- It is likely that a young person with autism will need support to master skills in the areas outlined in the triad of impairments as well as to manage sensory issues.

- Some young people will require low-arousal environments to process relevant information effectively.

Chapter 5

Types of Educational Provision

Most children attend their local mainstream school. Usually a child will go to the school nearest to him; indeed, it is one of the criteria used to select which pupils are offered a place. As a parent you can put forward a request for a particular school and this will be considered, but not guaranteed. You can express a preference for a school which is not the nearest to you, but the decision on securing a place will be made by the school. Issues that are considered include religious beliefs for faith schools, the number of places available, siblings attending the school and so on. You can request a full list of criteria from your LA. If you are seeking a place at a special school, the child will need to have a Statement and you will be offered a place at the school which can meet the needs outlined on the Statement and which is geographically the nearest to your home.

A number of students who attend mainstream school have a Statement but most children with autism in mainstream schools do not. Many parents want their child to attend mainstream school, particularly as the curriculum is designed for students who do not have a learning disability and may be more suitable for those children who have AS or HFA. Some mainstream schools also have specialist units within them for students with an ASD, which can give the specialist support required. The person within the school responsible for making sure that all children's SEN are met is the SENCO. Every school has a SENCO. In special schools it is often a role that the head teacher undertakes. It is advisable to meet with the SENCO if you feel that your child has SEN, whether a Statement is in place or not.

A mainstream school can refuse to take children with SEN in certain circumstances. They cannot turn the child down simply because he has SEN; however, they can refuse entry on the grounds that the school is unsuitable. The Education Act 1996 defines 'unsuitable' as being incompatible with the child's age, ability, aptitude or special educational needs, with the efficient education of the other children with whom the child would be educated, or with the efficient use of resources (Education Act 1996, section 27). Furthermore, the SEN Code of Practice (2001) states that

> An LEA that believes that the education of a particular child in the mainstream would be incompatible with the efficient education of others must consider whether there are any reasonable steps they could take to prevent the child's inclusion from having that effect. (DfES 2001, p.60, paragraph 8:58)

If this is the case and the school refuses admission, it may be that it is trying to help you and that your child may need more support than it can provide. It may even be able to give advice regarding a more suitable school placement. Assessment or further advice may be necessary to help you with this. The Qualifications and Curriculum Development Agency has further useful information on inclusion, including the Disability Discrimination Act 2005, which can be found on its website (see the Useful Websites at the end of this book for details).

There are various types of schools and they fall into one of the following seven categories:

- Foundation schools: governors have significantly greater responsibilities but also much greater freedom. They replaced grant-maintained schools in 1998.

- Trust schools: these are foundation schools with charitable status funded by the LA.

- Academies: these are directly funded by central government but may receive additional support from other sponsors. They are self-governing and most have charitable status but are still publicly funded.

- Grammar schools: these are a type of secondary school which is very focused on academic achievement.

- Voluntary aided schools: these schools are maintained by the LA but with a foundation (generally religious) which appoints some of the governing body. The site is usually owned by a charitable organisation.

- Voluntary controlled schools: the governing body is the employer and they will contribute towards the captial building costs. The site is normally owned by a charitable organisation.

- Maintained community schools: these are schools whose staffing, premises and admissions are the responsibility of the LA.

If a child's educational needs cannot be met in a mainstream setting there are a number of special schools which are maintained by the LA. Your child must have a Statement of SEN to be considered for a placement in a special school, and you can request a list of all special schools in your local area from the LA.

Special schools are designated to categories of special need. They are as follows:

LD (learning difficulties) Caters for a range of SEN including autism, although this depends on the severity.

MLD (moderate learning difficulties) Caters for a range of SEN including autism, although this depends on the severity.

SLD (severe learning difficulties) Caters for a range of SEN including autism, although this depends on the severity.

PD (physical disabilities)

BESD (behavioural, emotional and social disabilities)

AUTISTIC SPECTRUM (autism spectrum disorders)

PMLD (profound and multiple learning difficulties)

SpLD (specific learning difficulties) Caters for students with dyslexia.

There has been a definite trend for schools catering for specific disabilities to amalgamate and become more generic. This may suit your child; however, the environment and curriculum may not be autism-specific enough to meet the needs of some students. Check the designation of a school before visiting.

If you are looking for special school provision for your child, it is strongly advised that you visit the school and look for other pupils who have similar difficulties and diagnoses. It will be important that your child has an appropriate peer group and access to a curriculum that meets his needs. It is also important that your child can access any therapies he requires, preferably on the school campus so that therapists can be involved with teaching staff and parents in looking at environmental and curriculum issues. Try to keep your LA involved when seeking placement. It will be able to advise you on different schools that might meet your child's needs and will suggest you go and visit these. Your child's educational psychologist should be a key professional in helping decide which school would meet your child's needs.

You should be able to shortlist schools which may be suitable from the information that the LA sends you. Visit them and look at their Ofsted reports. These can be found on the Ofsted website (see Useful Websites section). There is a checklist that you may find useful to assess the extent to which a school engages with effective autism practice. This can be found in the Inclusion Development Programme on the Autism Spectrum which is on the National Strategies website (see Useful Websites section). Do not automatically assume that because a school has been designated for students with a specific disability such as autism it is necessarily going to be the most appropriate for your child. You need to consider your child's needs and which type of school is likely to meet these best. Every school will have a number of potential advantages and disadvantages and it is a case of weighing up which features are the most important for your child and your family. You can discuss with head teachers whether it is possible to modify aspects of their practice that might pose a difficulty. A sign of a good school is one where staff will discuss and consider such requests, rather than saying they are not able to make exceptions. By definition, children with SEN and autism will need some adjustments to what is provided for other children at the school – be it a special school or a mainstream school. It may be the case in some schools that the head teacher does not always have the capacity to make decisions about the pupils or the school as he is directed by the LA, a chief executive or a board of trustees to accept or not accept a child. Some focused questioning could reveal rather a lot if you go and visit.

If you find a school that you think is suitable, you will need to make a request to the LA for this school in Part 4 of the Statement. This request is taken to a panel of people within the LA who have to discuss the request and decide whether it is in the child's best interests and a fair use of the LA's limited resources. LAs do accept that some children with autism will be much more costly than others as some children have complex needs and serious difficulties in engaging in school life. Each LA has to ensure that resources are allocated fairly across all children and that those most in need get the most resources. Panels usually meet about every four to six weeks, and comprise a number of professionals such as teachers, psychologists and LA officers. They will discuss the request and make a judgement about whether your child's needs could be met in the school that you have proposed. This process is further examined later in this book. The LA is responsible for both mainstream and special 'maintained' schools.

If you feel that a maintained school cannot meet your child's needs, you may want to consider a school run by an independent organisation. This often has a residential element either because the children on roll are very demanding and their families are not able to manage them at home full time or because it is some distance from the child's home. Children might board at the school on a weekly basis, going home at the weekends, or on a termly basis, going home for holidays. In a few cases, the child might attend the school for 52 weeks of the year, going home for very few days in the year. This type of provision is therefore much more expensive than local day schools within the LA, and so the LA will look at all of its own schools in detail before agreeing to fund an out of county residential school.

Any school not maintained by the LA is referred to as an 'out of county placement', even if it happens to be in the county that you live in. You can request prospectuses directly from a school and you can send a copy of your child's paperwork to a school to seek that school's views on suitability prior to having a placement explored. You can also request that the LA send your child's paperwork to the school. The LA does not have to agree to this and may wish to send paperwork only to the schools that it has selected. Any school receiving paperwork will make a judgement about the suitability of the child. They are likely to want to meet with the child, usually at home and in his current school. If the school feels that the child may be suitable after meeting him, often the child will be asked to visit the school on an assessment basis. It is important to note that even if a school deems that it can meet your child's needs and offers a place, the LA may refuse to support the request or pay the fees. The high cost of placement will usually preclude parents from paying the fees themselves and most schools do not agree to accept funding directly from parents. It is important that you look at a range of provision prior to deciding on the most appropriate school for your child. As a rule of thumb, the more complex needs your child has the more specialist provision he is likely to require. Some mainstream schools have significantly changed their curriculum and the social and working environment to enable quite complex young people with autism to attend and to succeed there. Other mainstream schools are currently not able to do so, but the work of outreach teams and support from special school staff is enabling more mainstream primary and secondary schools each year to work effectively with children with autism. So in future, mainstream placement will be available and successful for a greater number of children with autism. It is not just academic or intellectual ability that decides whether a child goes to mainstream school or a special or specialist school; it is the extent to which his autism or the triad of impairment affects his ability to relate to other children and staff and to access the curriculum. Some children with autism, including those of above average ability with AS or who have been termed as having HFA, are so affected by it that they have not been able to sustain a place in a mainstream school and thus have been placed in a special school or a school or unit specific to children with an ASD. There are two or three specialist schools in the UK that specialise in teaching children with AS, for example.

If you and your LA agree that your child needs the very specialist provision that independent (residential) special schools can offer, including in-depth knowledge of the learning difficulty or syndrome, the high staff-to-pupil ratios, small classes and the residential element, your LA may well name a particular school or it may leave it up to you to find a school.

If you have found a few schools that seem suitable for your child, go and visit them. OAASIS (Office for Advice, Assistance, Support and Information on Special Needs) offers free advice leaflets on their website including a checklist of what to look for when visiting independent special schools. This can act as a useful aide memoire when viewing different schools and will help you to look beyond the building and its facilities.

Home schooling

Home schooling is another option that you may wish to consider. Be aware before embarking on this route that if you choose this path then you take on the responsibility from the LA to meet the needs of your child, and the Statement of SEN, if you have one, will no longer be legally enforceable.

It is absolutely legal for a parent to decide that home schooling may be a more appropriate source of education for his or her child rather than a school environment, and there are no obligations to have formal qualifications or training to undertake this role. There is also no requirement to have a structure to the day that mirrors that of a school, such as providing access to the NC and offering learning from 9 a.m. until 3.30 p.m. You are free to choose how to organise your child's education as long as you are offering 'suitable education'. However, you need to be aware that this can be very time-consuming and can be socially isolating for some children.

There are more than 20,000 families who educate their children at home and it can be very successful. However, in line with the *Every Child Matters* agenda, the government is now bringing out a compulsory registration scheme and will be able to refuse registration to home educate if there are safeguarding concerns. This may change with the new coalition government.

Education Otherwise (see Useful Websites section) is an organisation which can provide very useful information and structural support to families who home tutor. There are various methodologies that you may want to explore, such as Montessori or Steiner. On the whole children want to learn. There are halfway houses such as home school support centres around but be aware that if your child has SEN, you may not be qualified to give him the education which will meet his needs and allow him to reach his potential. Your child can, of course, return to a school at any time in the future.

You may be asked to provide the LA with information on the programme you have in place either via a home visit or by providing examples of work. Further information on home schooling can be found in the Useful Websites section at the back of this book.

KEY POINTS

- Most children attend their nearest mainstream school.

- Some children with Statements of SEN attend a mainstream school.

- There are certain circumstances which allow a mainstream school to turn down a request for admission from a student with SEN.

- Special schools are designated to categories of SEN.

- When seeking appropriate educational provision for your child things to look for include pupils with a similar profile of SEN, an appropriate peer group, an appropriate curriculum and access to therapeutic support on site.

- You must make a request to the LA if you wish any part of the Statement to be amended.

- Home schooling may be an option to consider.

Chapter 6

Educational Approaches and Programmes

There are many approaches that are used to educate and support young people with autism, and this can make it very tricky to decide which to use. To compound this there is little effective research into the success of individual programmes. Most schools use an eclectic mix of programmes, tailored to the specific needs of young people. A significant number of approaches are based on an understanding of the triad of impairment and aim to address specific difficulties which arise as a result of autism. All programmes and interventions should be based on a sound knowledge of the child and should take into account strengths and areas for development, as well as intellectual ability.

Some approaches are widely recognised and are used in whole or part in schools. They fall under the following broad categories: behavioural, interactive, communication and social interaction, Treatment and Education of Autistic and related Communication-handicapped Children (TEACCH), and Daily Life Therapy. There are also other interventions and strategies which may or may not be beneficial to individuals. They are further examined later in this chapter. It is likely that your child may benefit from an educational programme which incorporates an appropriate mix of these approaches and programmes, modified to suit his individual needs and learning style.

The curriculum offered should also be mindful that your child may have a limited understanding of other people's mental states and intentions, a focus on detail, problems in getting the gist of a situation or story and difficulties in organising himself and problem-solving. There may also be a need for sensory issues to be assessed and addressed, as well as other therapeutic support such as speech and language therapy (SaLT), clinical psychology, occupational therapy (OT) and subject-specific therapy such as art, music or drama.

Jordan *et al.* (1998) undertook a review of the rationale behind many of the most widely used approaches and examined the research available to support the effectiveness of these packages. More recently, in 2009, Parsons and colleagues updated this review (Parsons *et al.* 2009) and their report can be found at www.ncse.ie.

Behavioural approaches

These approaches are based on the theory that all behaviour is functional (that it serves a purpose such as to get one's needs met) and that skills can be taught which allow these needs to be met in a more appropriate way. The best-known form of this is Applied Behaviour Analysis (ABA). This technique defines unwanted or antisocial behaviours through observation and measures the frequency, severity and duration to provide a baseline. The baseline should serve to identify how much of a problem the behaviour is by providing clear data. A hypothesis about why the behaviour happens is then formed through a functional behavioural assessment which outlines whether the behaviour is happening because of a need to escape, to avoid or to get something tangible (such as some food), or whether it has an emotional basis (for example if the child is upset). Behaviours are analysed and antecedents (what happens before) as well as consequences (what the child gains from the behaviour) are fully investigated. New skills are taught to help the child to get his needs met as successfully as when he was engaging in the target behaviour. Furthermore, to reinforce positive attempts at engagement with desirable behaviours immediate rewards are offered.

Lovaas programmes were developed in the late 1960s by Dr O. Ivar Lovaas. The Lovaas approach consists of an intensive ABA programme for children which breaks down tasks into small steps (task analysis) and from this develops a daily programme to develop skills using positive reinforcement. This can be done as a home- or school-based programme. One significant part of this programme is the intensity of teaching and the number of people required to implement the programme. Few follow-up studies have been undertaken to ascertain the effectiveness of this programme in the long term, and some studies have suggested that it does not allow for generalisation to occur. Further details of this can be found using the Lovaas and Peach websites listed in the Useful Websites section at the end of this book.

Interactive approaches

These approaches aim to develop a relationship between the child and the person engaging with him. Only when a relationship has been established can other skills such as communication and social and emotional understanding be taught.

The playschool curriculum

This approach was developed in the USA in 1986 by Sally Rogers and colleagues for pre-school children. The aim of this is to increase cognition, symbolic understanding, communication, social and emotional understanding and interpersonal functioning. This is achieved using play, with the adult engaging at whatever level the child presents. The key here is the development of communication and relationships. The communication is often at a non verbal level and relies on signing and non verbal gesture. Social interaction is also instigated, at whatever level the child is functioning, leading to the adult making low-level demands on the child. The adult builds on positive behaviours displayed by the child rather than attempting to eradicate unwanted behaviours. Adults delivering this programme should be formally trained in this method.

The Infant Development Program

This was developed in the USA in 1997 by Geraldine Dawson and Julie Osterling to develop communication and cognition in young children with autism. It aims to put the child in charge of the communication. The adult imitates the child in an exaggerated but simplistic way. This allows communication to develop at the child's pace, and he can withdraw from it at any time. It promotes understanding of the purpose of communication in a non threatening and pleasurable way for the child.

Musical interaction therapy

This intervention was developed by staff working in a specialist school for children with ASD in the UK. Interactions between the child and his key worker or parent are supported by a musician at the keyboard or other instrument. It aims to develop communication and interaction skills through live music and play, and this can be done in a number of ways. The key worker can undertake a running commentary on what the child is doing through the medium of music and song and can encourage the child to take part in known songs, such as filling in a word after a pause or prompt. Often the key worker will use language relating to the activity being undertaken. The main thrust of this is the fact that it is child led, and skills and understanding are built upon as the sessions progress. Christie and colleagues have published a book on the approach (Christie *et al.* 2009).

Intensive interaction

This was developed by Melanie Nind and David Hewett in the 1980s as an approach for young people with autism, SLD and PMLD. It is mainly used with pre-verbal students and works on non verbal communication such as imitation, gesture and turn-taking. The person with autism is encouraged to lead and the facilitator imitates the non verbal communication. There is a vast amount of literature on this approach and its effectiveness (see Nind and Hewett 2005).

Option (Son-Rise) approach

This was an approach developed by Barry Kaufman in 1976, which Kaufman claimed had cured his son Raun of autism. It was designed specifically for children with autism and developmental disorders. Option works on the basis of engaging the child on his terms and mirroring the child's actions as a starting point. This then slowly shifts towards the therapist making low-level demands on the child. This programme is delivered at home by a group of therapists on a one-to-one basis and for this reason can be expensive and time-consuming. It also requires a room in the house to be dedicated to therapy.

Communication and social interactive approaches

These approaches aim to teach effective communication. They also aim to develop understanding of language and its content, as well as social interaction and social skills development.

Augmentative and alternative communication (AAC)

AAC is about parents and staff augmenting their methods of communication with the children – using objects, pictures, photos, symbols or words. It is not exclusive to children with autism; however, it can be very useful as an aid to teach functional communication and to foster language acquisition.

AAC can take the form of gesture (such as mimicking having a drink), signing (using Makaton or British Sign Language), eye pointing, using objects of reference (such as a plate to represent meal time) and many more. Adults can also use picture symbols to represent meaning, and this can be facilitated through the use of software programs such as Widgit. AAC also includes the use of different technologies, including computers, switches and voice synthesisers, for example. Further information on this method can be found in the Useful Websites section at the end of this book.

Facilitated communication

This method was initially used with students with cerebral palsy to try and help them control their fine motor movements but has since been used with a number of young people with autism. It is a means by which a person with communication impairment can be helped to use a keyboard to spell out what he wishes to say. This is aided by a facilitator who will guide the hand of the individual to develop pointing skills, the result being that a person with little functional speech or communication can interact with others. This is a highly controversial method which has attracted bad publicity as many research studies found that it was the adults who were communicating and not the child. Further information on this approach can be found on the NAS website.

Picture Exchange Communication System (PECS)

PECS was developed over 20 years ago in the USA as an augmentative communication system and has since received worldwide recognition. There is a detailed training manual supporting the implementation of this approach by Andy Bondy and Lori Frost (1994). It is, as the name would suggest, a system which helps to develop the transactional skills required in communication through the exchange of objects of reference or symbols. The child starts by using single word cards which have both a picture or symbol and the written word on them, and then is taught to make short phrases and sentences. This enables children with autism to communicate with others more effectively and it is suggested that behavioural problems reduce as a result and that it also encourages speech in some children.

Social Use of Language Programme (SULP)

SULP was developed and published by Wendy Rinaldi (1995). It has been used extensively in schools with children who have a wide range of language and communication disorders. It was found to be particularly good for young people with autism and this may be due to the very structured nature of the programme.

This approach caters for a wide range of ages from nursery to college and starts with the acquisition of basic skills in social language such as turn-taking, proxemics (how close you stand to someone when engaging with them), and rate, tone and volume (of speech). These are taught via games and stories with students having opportunities to practise and model the skills that they have been taught. This can help with generalisation of these skills.

The programme then develops more abstract skills such as making a friend, and winning and losing. This continues up to high-level skills such as acceptance of criticism. The programme is flexible and can be taught with the strengths and areas for development of the group leading the pace.

Hanen Program

The Hanen Centre offers autism-specific programmes to develop communication through family-focused programmes. The 'More than Words' programme uses everyday activities and play to develop skills in language and communication using predictability, structure and visual supports. Hanen also offers a programme called 'Talkability', which is aimed at enabling higher-functioning children aged three to seven to develop skills such as understanding non verbal cues and understanding how others feel. Further information on this approach can be found on the Hanen website.

Treatment and Education of Autistic and related Communication-handicapped Children (TEACCH)

This is one of the best-known approaches to support students with autism through structure, routine, organisation and predictability. Many schools adopt the rationale and strategies within TEACCH and modify these to suit their children and their environments.

It is a method of delivering highly structured teaching in a highly structured physical setting. It includes the use of individual detailed timetables with work systems to help students to access learning. This is aided by visual and written cues and clear direction as well as reinforcement and motivation.

This programme can be modified to support students in home settings and to meet the needs of all ages and abilities. There is a vast amount of information on this approach, including the Division TEACCH website.

Daily Life Therapy

This is an approach practised at the Higashi School in Boston, USA, which caters for students with autism from 3 to 22 years of age. It was developed by Dr Kiyo Kitahara and is based upon the ideology of seeking and attaining harmony in all aspects of life. It engages with the acquisition of harmony and balance by addressing group dynamics and modelling and physical activity, to achieve physically, emotionally and intellectually. It also supports the development of social independence and dignity. Their Physical Education curriculum is based upon the principles of sensory integration therapy. A socio-communicative approach to communication and language development is used.

Daily Life Therapy claims that the academic activity offered prepares students for inclusion opportunities. Some schools in the UK have started doing more physical activities during the day with children with autism (such as jogging, cycling and swimming) as a result of observing children at the school, as physical exercise appears to have a calming effect and to make the children ready for formal work. For further information visit their website (www.researchautism. net).

Other interventions and techniques

Not all programmes have an educational focus, and a number of interventions have been documented which may (or may not) be useful. As with all approaches you should look at the endorsements of others (and their background and perspective) and the level of intrusion that an approach may pose before attempting to put these in place. It will also be important that you question the validity of claims made against specific approaches and how well the intervention has been researched and assessed.

Auditory Integration Therapy (AIT)

This aims to correct auditory processing problems and involves sending high and low frequencies through headphones. There is some research that suggests that this programme can be helpful in desensitising some children to certain sounds and pitches; however, further research is required. More information can be found on the Berard AIT website (www.berardaitwebsite.com).

Dietary interventions

Some believe that an overgrowth of yeast can impact on the functioning of the central nervous system, causing pain and behavioural issues, and that all food containing yeast should be avoided. Other dietary interventions include identification of food intolerances such as milk, sugar and gluten. These intolerances may stop a person with autism being able to break down the protein peptides in these foods, which may cause toxins to leak into the blood and be transported to the brain. This, in theory, could cause pain and challenging behaviours. More research is required on the effectiveness of excluding certain foods from the diet of individuals with autism.

Melatonin

Melatonin is vital for sleep and some people believe that children with an ASD do not produce enough. Some believe that taking a supplement of melatonin may rectify this imbalance and help children with autism to go to sleep and stay asleep. It is used in the treatment of jet lag in the typical population. More research is needed into potential benefits and any side effects, but anecdotally some children have seemed to benefit from having melatonin as it often helps get them back into a healthy sleep routine. Then the melatonin can be discontinued.

Dolphin therapy and hippotherapy

Many establishments believe that swimming with dolphins can be therapeutic for people with autism. There are also a number of centres that believe that horse riding and horse management (hippotherapy) may be beneficial. This may be because it offers an approach to sensory integration problems. Many children enjoy horse riding and as they need to give their attention to the horse and the riding, their anxiety and other sensory issues might be reduced, that is, they are distracted from other concerns.

Irlen lenses

This involves the use of tinted glasses to improve visual perception and the use of coloured overlays to aid reading. It is based on the assumption that some people with autism have visual perception problems which can lead to visual distortions. Some people with autism have said that they cannot see faces clearly but have been able to do so when wearing coloured lenses, or that these lenses have improved their ability to see and read text.

As you can see, a huge number of approaches and programmes can be used to support young people with an ASD. It can be a minefield to find the right one for an individual, and establishments may favour one approach over another. When developing bespoke packages for young people it is important to start with their strengths and weaknesses and build approaches around this. For example, if you are working with a young person who appears to like order and consistency a modified TEACCH approach could work well. If the child has good speech but poor social understanding then it may be worth looking at SULP. The important thing to understand is that you can take the most appropriate parts of a number of programmes and create a unique approach which supports the needs and motivational interests of individuals. The most recent research would suggest that the most effective programmes are based upon routine, structure and predictability.

When developing any type of programme it will be important that there is an element of reward. This leads to the question of whether a young person's area of special interest should be used. It may be that there is a concern that special interests can be difficult to manage, or that they dominate the young person's thinking. I believe that if you can place boundaries around the special interest then it can be a useful tool to motivate the young person to engage. A boundary might be that the young person can talk to a known adult about his obsession with trains for 30 minutes each evening between 6 and 6.30 p.m. A special interest does form part of an individual's unique personality, and on this level it would be very sad and not helpful to remove it. However, if a special interest is hindering social engagement or social interaction, or is becoming dangerous then obviously it will need to be modified.

There are huge whole-school training issues around the development of appropriate programmes for young people with ASD. It is imperative that teachers and support staff understand the child and the impact that his autism has on processing and acquisition of skills and knowledge. It is also vital that staff understand the rationale behind individual approaches. If they don't, they will not be able to modify and develop programmes in line with the child's response to these. It is also vital that staff who do not teach, but who come into contact with pupils with autism, are trained to create an autism-friendly environment. Finally, it is also useful for a school to undertake peer awareness training and develop supports such as Circle of Friends (Whitaker *et al.* 1998) or buddy systems.

KEY POINTS

- There is a vast range of approaches and programmes used with young people with autism and these are often based on the triad of impairment.

- Programmes broadly fall into the following categories: behavioural, interactive, communication and social interaction, TEACCH and Daily Life Therapy.

- The most effective programmes are usually based on an eclectic mix of approaches.

- There is also a range of interventions and techniques used which do not generally form part of an educational programme.

Chapter 7

How to Find an Appropriate Specialist School

This section may be useful if your child has been assessed and found to have an ASD (possibly with a learning disability) and you are looking for an appropriate specialist educational establishment to meet his needs. Remember that you must have secured a Statement for this to be a consideration. You must have the agreement of the LA that your child requires a very specialist setting or funding for this will not be forthcoming and it is unlikely that you would have the means to pay for this privately, as schools can range in cost from £20,000 per child per year for a day place to in excess of £400,000 per child per year for a 52-week residential school.

A major consideration when choosing a school is whether a residential school is required. It may be that your child will require this to have his educational needs met or that the family is under extreme pressure and really struggles to manage their child when he is at home. In this case health and social care will need to agree that the needs are such that residential schooling should be explored and if that is the case, then they would share the funding for the child with education.

This decision of what type of school is required is reached in consultation with the LA, who will first look at all of the provision that they maintain. It may also look at provision which is in a neighbouring county but is still maintained by an LA. It will look at this option as it may be closer and is almost certainly going to be less expensive. Few authorities have residential schools so they may try to put together a package of short-term care and/or foster care to keep the young person within the county. If you believe that the only successful option is a specialist residential school it will be up to you to put forward reasons why other types of provision would be unsuccessful at meeting your child's SEN. Remember that the LA will only look at the child's *educational* needs when deciding on provision. It will not take into account the needs of other family members such as siblings or the impact that your child may be having on family life. Health needs such as severe epilepsy will be taken into consideration, and this type of placement is referred to as a dual fund (part funded by the LA and part funded by health). Social needs can also be taken into consideration if there is agreement that this is a significant factor affecting educational needs and in this instance social care would be responsible for part of the fees.

Occasionally all three departments are deemed to be jointly responsible and this is referred to as a tri part fund. The LA is still the most likely body to manage the placement, but this will be in conjunction with other departments. As a parent you will have no input into who pays the fees, and the LA remains legally responsible for meeting the SEN as outlined in your child's Statement, even if the provision detailed is under the remit of health or social care. If a child is placed in a residential school he is then classed as a looked after child (LAC). This does not mean that you lose parental responsibility for him; rather it means that the placement is monitored by social care and that a nominated officer (usually a social worker) will visit the child and inspect the school premises on a regular basis to check the school are meeting the child's care needs.

Once it has been agreed by the LA that your child requires a residential placement, it is likely that you will be informed of the type of provision that will be funded. This is likely to be weekly boarding (38 week) or termly boarding (44 week or 52 week). It is important to establish this prior to seeking out a school, although of course you may disagree and look at provision which you think is more suitable prior to presenting this to the LA. If weekly boarding has been agreed then your child will come home every weekend. There is obviously a transport issue here, and the LA should be responsible for providing appropriate transport to and from the school. In tribunal cases, parents sometimes waive their right to transport in order to secure the school that they have nominated, as transport costs can be very costly to authorities. Sometimes children are placed in weekly boarding schools simply because of the distance from the school to home (as a rule of thumb if the journey takes more than one hour each way). It may be that your child does not need a residential element but requires very specialist teaching and support, so these schools will usually take one or two children on a daily basis from home if they live close enough.

If termly boarding is agreed the child may still come home on a regular basis (such as every two or three weeks). Again this needs to be agreed with your LA as there is a cost implication. Those children who take up 52-week boarding places can also visit home on a regular basis, although some children remain at school all year and parents and siblings visit them at the school. Again this would be a decision that would be made in light of need.

Your LA may furnish you with a list of schools which it would like you to consider. These will have been chosen on locality, specialism and cost. Initially it may be worth looking at the schools' websites as this will give you an idea of whether they may be suitable. It is likely that you will be able to rule some out immediately, for example if they do not cater for the needs outlined on your child's Statement, or if the staff-to-pupil ratio is not high enough. It may be that you have requested a rural site as your child requires space and will run off if anxious. If there are any schools that you feel may be suitable, you can give them a call and request a visit. If there are no schools put forward by the LA, or they are all inappropriate, then you will have to find one yourself. The internet is likely to be the best way to do this. There are many good sites which will help you to narrow down your search. The Independent Special Boarding International site is good (www.isbi.com) as is the NAS site (www.nas.org.uk) and Schoolsnet (www.schoolsnet.com). Other sites worth looking at are the Department for Education and Skills (DfES) EduBase (www.edubase.gov.uk) and the Independent Schools Council (www.isc.co.uk). All links are duplicated in the Useful Websites section at the end of this book. Another good source of information is Gabbitas, an educational consultancy which produces an annual guide to schools catering for special needs. This can be purchased via its website (www.gabbitas.co.uk). The NAS also produces a book which lists schools, units and classes for children with autism and AS, which and can be found on its website.

If your child is over 16 years of age, there are two guides which may help you to find a suitable educational establishment. One is called 'COPE' and is available from Orca Book Services, and the other is the Association of National Specialist Colleges (NATSPEC). This is free and details can be found in the Useful Websites section of this book.

Prior to choosing a school make sure that you have read the most recent Ofsted report. This will tell you how well the school is performing and areas in which it has to improve. The reports can be obtained directly from the school, or you can visit the Ofsted website and view reports from any school which is Ofsted registered. Most LAs will not fund placement at a school which does not have this registration so it is worth bearing this in mind.

In 2007, the Commission for Social Care Inspection (CSCI) became the Care Quality Commission (CQC) and Ofsted took over the monitoring of health and social care (the boarding part of residential education). Ofsted reports now include the effectiveness of boarding provision as well as academic achievement. In 2009 the framework for Ofsted was amended, placing more emphasis on improving outcomes for young people and safeguarding issues. Schools are now inspected under this new framework and are given an overall grade which ranges from 1 (outstanding) to 4 (inadequate). The reports contain advice to the school as to what it must do to improve further. It also contains the views of parents and carers which may be of interest. Obviously if a school has a low grade then it must be approached with caution as to the quality of what it offers.

In terms of what to look at, I would suggest that you compile a list which can be used to compare schools. It is unlikely that a school will have absolutely everything that your child wants; however, it should have everything that your child needs. Once you have narrowed your search down to a handful of schools it is important to visit with a checklist in mind. It is easy to get sidetracked by the large stately home and the beautifully manicured grounds and miss some of the pivotal details that could severely impact on the quality of life, safety and well-being of your child. Most parents get a gut feeling about an environment and if it would be a place that they could see their child.

You may wish to consider some of the following when visiting a school:

Education

- How has the curriculum been modified or developed to meet the children's needs?
- Do lessons follow a predictable routine?
- Are children given opportunities to practise skills learned in the classroom in real-life settings?
- How many pupils are in each class?
- What is the staff-to-pupil ratio?
- Are pupils expected to do homework?
- Does the school use a key worker approach?
- How does the school address issues around bullying?
- Does the school have access to advocates?
- How many computers and other IT aids are in each class?
- How is the school governed?

Care

- How often are pupils taken into the community?
- Is there a life skills curriculum and if so, how is this delivered?
- Are there arrangements in place for children to access clubs outside of the school?
- Are the bedrooms personalised?
- Are there any night staff who remain awake?
- Is there a policy about intimate care?
- How much choice is offered at mealtimes?
- Does the school cater for special diets?
- How often do the pupils shower or bathe?
- Who provides the toiletries and uniform?
- What procedures are in place to do laundry?

- What activities are offered in the evening or at weekends?

- Is there a designated space for parents to spend time with their child on site?

- Can parents stay overnight at the school?

- Can pupils have TV/laptop/games in their room?

- What time do pupils go to bed and get up?

Staffing

- What sort of training is offered to staff and how frequently?

- How is information about pupils given to staff?

- How do the education staff and residential staff share information?

Therapeutic and medical support

- How are the sensory needs of pupils managed?

- Does the school have a speech and language therapist?

- Does the school have an occupational therapist?

- Can children access psychiatric/psychological support if required in a timely fashion?

- How does the school manage dental visits?

Other

- How many other students have the same disability as your child?

- Does the school have clear policies on behaviour support and use of restraint?

- How frequently are children's plans updated?

- How close is the nearest town/swimming pool/library?

- How are parents kept informed about their child?

- Can pupils access a telephone whenever they want to?

- What is the ratio of boys to girls?

- What safeguarding measures are in place for pupils who run off?

Some residential schools offer a service whereby they can put you in touch with other parents who have children at the school. This can be useful in assessing how the school interacts with parents, and how easy it is to get to speak to relevant staff during the day, evening and weekends.

For further guidance on how good practice is measured, the DfES has a guide for staff working with students with autism to use as a self-evaluation tool. The link to this can be found in the Useful Websites section at the end of this book.

Once you feel that you have found the right school you need to liaise with your LA outlining the reasons that you feel that this particular school could meet your child's needs. Most schools will want a formal request from the LA to consider your child. This will involve looking at the Statement and appendices as well as the last annual review. If the LA refuses to approach a school formally then you may wish to talk to the head teacher about the possibility of appealing the decision.

If the school has a vacancy in the right year group with an appropriate peer group it is likely to assess the child formally both in the educational setting and at home. Some schools like potential students to spend some time at the school so that they are able to see how they would fit in. Other schools, however, may conclude that this would be too stressful for the child. Once the child is offered a place a full transition plan is usually drawn up which details exactly what will happen next.

KEY POINTS

- If seeking a residential school you must be clear about the reasons for this. It may be because your child needs this for educational reasons, or it could be due to health and social needs.

- Transport can be a highly significant cost and this needs to be included in the funded package.

- The LA may advise you regarding schools that it wishes you to consider. If you believe them to be unsuitable be clear about why this is the case.

- Make a list of what you are going to look at and consider when visiting different schools.

- Assessment of your child is likely to take place in a range of settings.

Chapter 8

~~~~~~~~

How to Work Effectively with Outside Agencies

Any parent will know that there is a huge range of people and outside agencies that support your child in one way or another. There is a government shift towards agencies dealing with young people to offer a more joined up and integrated approach and this has been particularly true since the *Every Child Matters* agenda was published. The number of agencies working with children with disabilities can be even greater, and this demands an even more integrated approach to be effective, whereby information is shared and approaches and plans are understood by all involved.

Traditionally, multi-agency working has not been without its issues. The model that has historically supported children with SEN is that of education, health and social care. For children with complex needs all three agencies have had a part to play in the support and care of these young people; however, this has created tensions and not just in the area of funding. To begin with, the language that is used by one agency is not necessarily understood by the others. All three agencies are known for their overuse of abbreviations and acronyms, and this can be highly confusing for parents and professionals alike. All agencies want their opinion to form the basis of a child's programme but there is often a tension around the primary need and how best to support and develop a child. For example, an educationalist may believe that modification of behaviour would be best achieved through the teaching of new skills and knowledge via the curriculum, whereas a clinical psychologist may believe that changes in behaviour may only happen through cognitive behavioural therapy. A speech and language therapist may believe that a child's communication and language are so deviant that without the development of functional communication it would be impossible to modify behaviour. In truth, most agencies have a significant part to play and a multi-layered approach to support tends to be the most effective one.

In dealing with such a range of specialist services understanding the role and responsibilities of each one can become confusing. This is further compounded when funding issues come into play. It may be that your child requires specialist educational provision because of severe medical needs or because of social needs. It would be realistic then to assume that the appropriate agency would be responsible for the fees for this, and that decisions around placement would lie with them. This is not the case, as educational provision tends to have an educationalist taking the lead on identification. This has led to tension between the different agencies as recommendations may be made by health, for example, which are set against the budgets of other agencies.

The Common Assessment Framework (CAF) was introduced to try to bring all of these agencies together and help multi-agency working practices as part of the ECM agenda. It was intended to give a voice to parents and children in the development of a plan to make sure that the young person gets the right support and help, and to these ends the plan should include the views of the child and the family. The CAF forms an assessment of the core needs of a young person with SEN and should be completed by a lead professional. This person can be anyone who understands the additional needs of the child and he will then become responsible for the management and monitoring of the recommendations. The plan should identify everyone involved with the child and specifically state if the child needs extra support and if so who should provide it. The significant part of the introduction of this form of assessment is seeing parents as equal partners in the process. Parental views need to be considered and parents need to be involved in decision-making. Children with complex needs may already have a lead professional and it may be that a CAF is not appropriate as the child has had specialist assessment through statutory frameworks.

The development of a CAF should bring together a Team Around the Child (TAC), which is a group of multi-disciplinary professionals specifically formed to help and support the young person. This team may not have previously worked together; however they should provide information, guidance and advice to the lead professional. They should also be responsible and accountable for fulfilling their agreement of delivery of services and support to the young person.

Other developments that have happened in line with the ECM agenda in the drive to support better multi-disciplinary working practices are working groups which identify and plan how the needs of young people and their families will be met. There is now a statutory requirement for a Children and Young People's Plan (CYPP) to be developed, its aims being better integration of children's services, the strengthening of partnership arrangements and identification of improvements to be made. This, in essence, should be a child-centred, outcome-led vision for all children and young people which is clearly informed by their views and those of the families. The responsibility for preparation, publication and revision of this plan has recently been transferred from the LA to Children's Trust Boards.

These developments must be seen as a step in the right direction in terms of getting a child's needs met; however, these directives are not always adhered to and some authorities are still trying to unpick what good practice looks like and who ultimately is responsible and therefore accountable.

The Lamb Report (DCSF 2010) was commissioned to look at SEN and parental confidence in the system. It is an extremely interesting report which outlines the views of parents in the process of securing services for their child. It recommends that a major reform to the current system is required with change in the following key areas: outcomes for children should be at the heart of the system; parents should have a stronger voice; there needs to be a system with a greater focus on children's needs; and there should be a more accountable system that delivers better services. Interestingly, the report states that the spirit of the current framework is adequate but it falls down with its failure to comply.

As a parent it is very difficult to maintain effective working relationships with a variety of people who may try and pass responsibility to others around them. It can be confusing and frustrating. It is important that you remember the role that the LA plays in identifying educational provision and how funding streams work. It is advisable to try to work with your LA in a non threatening manner, making use of the PPS which are in place. Keep your LA informed about what you are doing, and make sure that it is copied in to any letters that you send (or receive). Try to have a named officer with whom you can correspond, and I would suggest that you do this in writing to create a paper trail of requested events and outcomes. It is also extremely important that you work closely with the school. You may think that it is not meeting your child's needs; however, it is likely to be doing everything that it can to do so.

If you can, try to wade through the SEN Code of Practice, as it contains vital information about the rights of your child. You will be surprised how many educationalists you will encounter who have not understood or do not follow the guidelines laid out. Try to refer to it without being confrontational. No one likes to be criticised, so try to have positive things to say to the school as well as suggestions for improvements.

The other area which can be a minefield in terms of securing support is short-term care. This should be done via social care, but, as is true with other agencies, they have tight budgets and even tighter criteria for assistance. If you are turned down in your request for help you are entitled to ask for the criteria used to select those who will be given short-term care. Don't be shy about asking for help with care or explaining that you are not coping and need some support. No one will think badly of you and your child will benefit more in the long run if you are able to manage the situation effectively.

The Aiming High for Disabled Children (ADHC) agenda (2007) is an initiative jointly led by the Department for Children, Schools and Families (DCSF) and the Department of Health (DH). It is directly aligned to the Being Healthy outcome detailed in the ECM agenda. The core offer is set up to provide resources (including funding) for a number of activities including short breaks for disabled children and childcare. You should have a local group that meets and considers requests for support. You can find out more about this initiative at the DCSF website, and details of your local group should be found on your LA website. This funding currently has less than a year to go, although it may be replaced with another form of support.

When requesting help in the form of short breaks you may be offered a befriender, or 'buddy', who is someone who will take your child to an activity he enjoys such as swimming or visiting the library or park. You may be offered an overnight break in a short-break centre or with a foster family. It is important that you talk over the options and understand the differences between these types of support. Check if you are able to interview the person assigned to you, as in many cases you can. Also make sure that you are given a suitable introductory period where the befriender can spend time with you present, getting to know your child and making sure that they are going to form an appropriate friendship. All people who work with your child more than once a week have to undergo formal Criminal Records Bureau (CRB) checks.

If you are eligible for short breaks but no carer can be found you are entitled to ask that a budget be given to you by which you can employ someone independently. This is referred to as Direct Payments. Be mindful that by doing this you are entering into an employment contract with someone, which may be more complex than it appears. Also note that this can include another member of your family or a friend if they are approved and do not live with you.

If you feel that a residential school is required for your child because of his social needs it will be important to have secured short-break care to indicate the level of need. This will be particularly important if the current school feels that it is meeting educational needs. Talk to your child's current school about its out-of-school clubs and extended school activities as this may also help.

In summary, working with outside agencies can be a real struggle for parents, and you may not always agree with their opinions. However, it is in your and your child's best interests to engage as effectively with staff and other agencies as you can, so that you are able to secure the most appropriate support.

KEY POINTS

- The government has issued directives to support greater multi-agency working. In practice this is not without its issues.

- Education tends to take the lead on the identification and monitoring of residential schooling even if there is more than one funding stream.

- The CAF can be useful in identifying additional needs that your child may have as well as who is responsible and accountable for the delivery of additional services.

Chapter 9

The SEN Code of Practice

The revised SEN Code of Practice took effect in January 2001, superseding the previous version. Its recommendations are not written in law; however, an LA and therefore a school must 'have regard' to this Code when carrying out its duties towards all pupils with SEN. It was revised in light of the Disability Discrimination Act 1995, the Education Act 1996, the Human Rights Act 1998 and the SEN and Disability Act 2001. Since the Code was issued Local Education Authorities (LEAs) are now referred to as Local Authorities. They are the same body of people and have the same legally binding obligation to make available the provision as outlined in the Statement of SEN. The LA has ultimate legal responsibility for meeting needs although it devolves this responsibility to the schools.

To have an idea of what constitutes a SEN, the Code states that a child with a SEN may need *additional or different* help from that given to other children of the same age'. A full copy of this document can be found following the link given in the Useful Websites section at the end of this book.

The fundamental principles of the Code are:

- a child with SEN should have his needs met

- the SEN of children will normally be met in mainstream or early education settings

- the views of the child should be sought and taken into account

- parents have a vital role to play in supporting their child's education

- children with SEN should be offered full access to a broad, balanced and relevant education, including an appropriate curriculum for the foundation stage and the NC.

It also states that:

- there should be flexibility to allow a child who does not have a Statement to attend a special school in exceptional circumstances

- in some instances a child does not have to go through the varying levels of help before a request for formal assessment is made

- a school can request a Statutory Assessment.

The Code outlines a model of graduated help which may lead to the issuing of a Statement:

- differentiated learning

- School Action or Early Years Action if the child is aged between three and five

- School Action Plus or Early Years Action Plus

- Statutory Assessment

- Statement of SEN.

Differentiated learning

This is the way that teachers can modify an activity or task to help a child understand it. This may be by changing the language or by breaking down the task into smaller steps to make it achievable.

School Action

This is where subject teachers or SENCOs identify that a pupil has a SEN, and devise interventions '*additional to or different from* those provided' as part of the school's usual differentiated curriculum. The child will usually get an Individual Education Plan (IEP) which will list the nature of the difficulties, short-term targets, teaching strategies, provision and review date. It should be discussed with the parents and reviewed regularly.

School Action Plus

The SENCO and subject/pastoral staff, in consultation with parents, ask for help from external services (such as therapists) to get advice and support and help to set new targets. If there is still a concern after these steps have been taken a Statutory Assessment should be requested. This will mean that the school does not believe it is able to meet fully the child's needs.

Statutory Assessment

As a parent you can also request that a Statutory Assessment is carried out under Section 328 or 329. You may do this if the school disagrees with you. Independent Parental Special Education Advice (IPSEA) is a group which supports parents with educational issues and it has template letters which you can download from its website to send via the school. The LA must respond to this request and must inform the child's head teacher, unless it has made a Statutory Assessment within six months of the date requested or has concluded that a Statutory Assessment is not necessary.

Fundamentally, the Code strengthened the right to a place in mainstream school for children with SEN, except when it affects the 'efficient education' of other children. Parents also have a right to state a preference for a special school, although they are not automatically entitled to this. The LA can refuse this request if it feels that it is not an efficient use of its resources. The school has a duty to inform parents that SEN provision is being made for the child because the child has SEN.

Statement

If the LA agrees to undertake a Statutory Assessment this may lead to the agreement that a child requires a Statement of SEN. If this is the case, a draft Statement will be sent to you for your agreement. It may be that you do not agree with the LA decision or the content of the Statement. You may appeal this.

There is a legal requirement to offer PPS and these are set out in the Education Act 1996.

> A local education authority must arrange for the parents of any child in their area with special educational needs to be provided with advice and information about matters relating to those needs.

> A local education authority must make arrangements with a view to avoiding or resolving disagreements between authorities (on the one hand) and parents of children in their area (on the other) about the way LEAs and maintained schools carry out their responsibilities towards children with special educational needs.

> A local authority must also make arrangements with a view to avoiding or resolving disagreements between parents and certain schools about the special educational provision made for their child. (Education Act 1996, Section 332A/332B 1 and 2)

Every LA has a PPS and details of these can be found on the PPS website. The Code also gives guidance on resolving disagreements, and this is part of the legal requirements also set out in the Education Act 1996.

The Code offers guidance to the LA pertaining to the writing of a Statement. Again the LA must 'have regard' to these recommendations.

Part 2 should clearly and thoroughly describe a child's current difficulties, setting out the nature and severity of these.

Part 3 should specify all the provision to be made with long-term objectives. The LA must specify facilities, equipment, staffing arrangements and modifications to the curriculum including exclusions and substitutions. Provision required should be specific and quantifiable and it must also state if residential accommodation is needed.

Part 4 of the Statement should be left blank at the proposal stage; however, in the final Statement the type of school should be specified or the provision for education other than at school.

Part 5 should specify non educational needs such as therapeutic support.

Part 6 must specify non educational provision.

Where parental advice has been received, the LA should always make reference in Part 2 to at least one piece of information from this.

When writing advice to inform the Statement this must not be influenced by consideration of a particular school at which the child may eventually be placed. Specific schools must not be suggested.

The Code also states the importance of finding out the ascertainable wishes and feelings of the child and involving him when decisions are made which affect him. This can be in expressing a preference for a particular school. It is advisable to arrange to take a child along to any school which you are aware that the LA is likely to suggest as 'suitable' so that you have first-hand evidence to support any problems that he is likely to encounter.

Guidance is given on preparation and conducting reviews in the Code. They should happen at least once a year and they should be a review of the Statement. An interim review can be called when a child is at serious risk of exclusion, when a child has needs that are known to change rapidly or when there is a disagreement between parents and professionals. The LA should review the Statement in light of the head teacher's report and decide whether to amend it or cease to maintain it. Wherever possible the pupil should be invited to the review. The LA must write to the parents informing them of the decisions taken regarding the Statement and the reasons for these decisions.

The Code of Practice is frequently referred to in tribunal, and there have been a number of cases which have further defined what this means in practice. It is strongly advised that you make yourself aware of the content of the Code if you are seeking specialist educational provision for your child.

KEY POINTS

- An LA must 'have regard' to the Code whilst carrying out its duties to all pupils with SEN.

- Fundamental principles are that a child with SEN will have his needs met, normally in a mainstream school. The views of the child and family will be sought and the curriculum should be appropriate.

- There is a model of graduated help starting with differentiation leading to a Statutory Assessment.

- PPS can help with the process as well as providing advice and support.

- The Code outlines how a Statement should be written and what should be in each part.

- The Code also outlines requirements regarding annual reviews.

Chapter 10

The Process of Securing a Statement of SEN

If your child has a problem which is preventing him from progressing either academically or socially the school will look at a graduated approach to helping him. The steps involved are listed in the previous chapter. If the school has put in place all of these steps and still feels that there is a problem then they should request a Statutory Assessment of SEN. This can lead to the issuing of a Statement of SEN, or an amendment of a Statement of SEN which is a legally enforceable document outlining the nature of the child's SEN and the provision required. As a parent you can also request a Statutory Assessment of Need (or reassessment if a Statement has already been issued).

The Education Act 1996 states that a child is considered to have SEN if he

1. has a significantly greater difficulty in learning than the majority of children the same age; or

2. has a disability which prevents or hinders him from making use of educational facilities of a kind generally provided for children of the same age in schools within the area of the LEA (Local Education Authority). (Education Act 1996, Section 312)

If you are concerned about your child you should discuss this with the school and seek its views.

If you are requesting a Statutory Assessment you will need evidence to support this. It could be that your child is not making progress in his current setting or that other professionals have reported that your child has a SEN. You will need to write a letter to your LA, usually to the Head of Children's Services. The letter also will need to be copied to the school. A template letter and a format for writing a report about your child can be found on the Advisory Centre for Education (ACE) website. If the school or other professional approaches the LA for an assessment you will be informed.

Once the LA has received your request it has six weeks in which to decide either to assess or not. If you have not already done so you will be asked to provide evidence as to why you think your child needs a Statutory Assessment or reassessment. You should at this point be provided with details of your local PPS. If an LA takes longer than six weeks, you should ask your named officer to explain the delay. If you are not happy with the answer or the reason for the delay, you can talk to the local PPS or ask the LA to arrange to sort out the disagreement informally through an independent person. As a last resort you can complain to the Secretary of State for Children, Schools and Families about any unreasonable delay. The Secretary of State can tell the LA to inform you whether they will be carrying out a Statutory Assessment.

In deciding whether to assess, the LA will look at what the school has done to address your child's SEN and if anything further could be put in place to allow your child to remain in his current school. You can provide the LA with independent private reports, but be mindful of timeframes if you are going to commission these for the purpose of convincing the LA to assess. It can take months to arrange private assessments with independent SaLTs, educational psychologists, clinical psychologists, psychiatrists and OTs. They can also be extremely costly (at the time of writing, up to £1000 per report).

If your child receives a diagnosis of an LD from an independent assessment centre or consultant, the report you receive does not have to be used by your LA when it is deciding whether or not to make a formal assessment. It will, however, indicate that experts believe that your child may have a problem, and copies of any such reports should be sent to your LA if you are requesting an assessment. If the LA decides to carry out a formal assessment then the LA educational psychologist should consider these reports. Parents can also ask for other appropriate advice to be considered. Keep copies of everything you send, and don't forget to date your letters.

If the LA agrees to assess, it will usually arrange for the child to be seen in school by an educational psychologist. Information may also be sought from teachers, health professionals and social care. They have ten weeks in which to complete the assessment. They must decide at the end of ten weeks if they are going to issue a Statement or amend an existing one.

Within two weeks of the decision, the LA must let you know if it does not intend to issue or amend a Statement, or let you have the proposed Statement. It may be that the LA decides to issue a note in lieu which can look very much like a Statement as it may broadly follow the format of a Statement; however, this is not a legally enforceable document.

If a proposed Statement is issued then parents have the right to state a preference for a school usually via a meeting with the LA. If a parent wishes to name a school which is different from that in the proposed Statement they must do so within 15 days. The final Statement should be issued within eight weeks of the proposed Statement.

If you do not agree with the LA decision at any point, or if you do not agree with the named school in the final Statement you have a right of appeal to the First Tier Tribunal for SEND. The LA will inform you of the timeframe for lodging this appeal and will advise you of your right to mediation through the SEN Disagreement Resolution Service.

If a Statement is issued it must be in the form prescribed in the Code of Practice. All advice obtained and taken into consideration must be attached as appendices to the Statement, and the wording of the Statement should be clear and unambiguous. Part 4 of the Statement must be left blank at the proposal stage.

Case law has established that speech and language therapy can be regarded as either educational or non educational. However, addressing speech and language impairments should normally be recorded as educational provision unless there are exceptional reasons for not doing so. The Statement should advise on the nature and extent of provision and how this would best be delivered (e.g. individually or in groups). It should advise who delivers the provision and how it will be monitored and assessed. It should clearly quantify the nature of the provision in hours and delivery.

The Statement should not have provision which states such things as 'access to' or 'when required' as these are non measurable. Check the draft Statement to make sure that this is not the case. Don't be afraid to send it back with your own views on what it should include or those of the professionals employed by you who have made recommendations. These details will be vital to securing the level of education which your child needs.

If the LA names a residential provision which is some distance from your home it should provide transport or travel assistance. The LA is legally responsible for providing the support outlined in the Statement until he is 19 years old, or until he leaves school. The Statement can be maintained until 19 if it is agreed that the child should stay at the school post 16. The Statement ceases to be valid if the child moves to a local sector college funded by the Learning and Skills Council (LSC), which has recently been renamed the Young People's Learning Agency (YPLA).

Parents often find it useful to build up a file of documentation dated and in chronological order. It can be a very time-consuming task to put this together after the event. It also ensures that important documentation does not get lost.

If you do not agree with the decision of the LA you have a right of appeal to the Upper Tribunal, and you may wish to engage legal representation to support you with this. It can sometimes be useful to have legal support from the request stage; however, you need to make sure that you communicate effectively with the LA from the beginning. There are also a number of organisations which may be able to support and guide you through the process. These can be found in the Useful Websites section at the end of this book.

Timeline and order of events

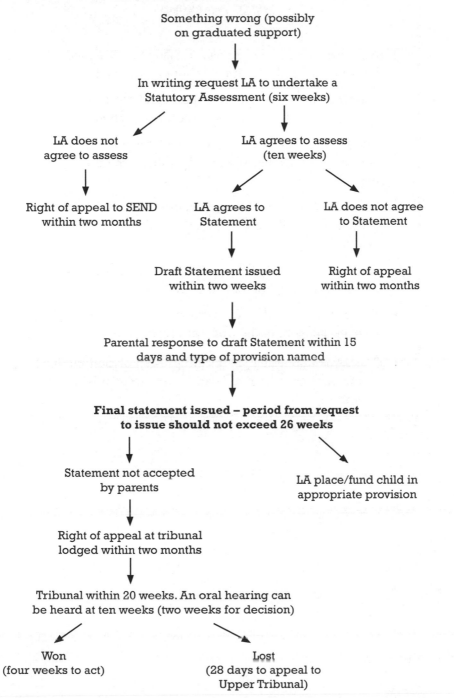

Something wrong (possibly on graduated support)

↓

In writing request LA to undertake a Statutory Assessment (six weeks)

LA does not agree to assess

LA agrees to assess (ten weeks)

Right of appeal to SEND within two months

LA agrees to Statement

LA does not agree to Statement

Draft Statement issued within two weeks

Right of appeal within two months

Parental response to draft Statement within 15 days and type of provision named

↓

Final statement issued – period from request to issue should not exceed 26 weeks

Statement not accepted by parents

LA place/fund child in appropriate provision

Right of appeal at tribunal lodged within two months

↓

Tribunal within 20 weeks. An oral hearing can be heard at ten weeks (two weeks for decision)

Won (four weeks to act)

Lost (28 days to appeal to Upper Tribunal)

KEY POINTS

- As a parent you can request a Statutory Assessment or reassessment by the LA if the school refuses to do so.

- You will require evidence to support and substantiate your reasons for wanting an assessment for your child.

- The LA will look at what the school has done to address your child's SEN and if anything further could be put in place.

- You can commission private reports on your child, and consideration will be given to them if the LA decides to assess.

- Children will usually be assessed in school, but you will be informed and your views will be sought.

- Statements should be written in line with the recommendations in the Code of Practice.

- The LA is responsible for meeting the provision outlined in the Statement, and it devolves this responsibility to a school.

Chapter 11

SEN Law and SEND Tribunals

From 3 November 2009, SENDIST ceased to be a standalone body and became part of a new two-tier structure. What this means in practice is that the two new tiers work with other groups dealing with similar issues such as those occurring in health and social care. The existing judges and staff of SENDIST transferred to the new two-tier system so their work continues in much the same way with some slightly amended rules. The First Tier Tribunal is now called SEND, and appeals against SEND are now heard by the Upper Tribunal instead of the High Court.

The First Tier Tribunal will hear all appeals against LAs in England, and will form part of the Health, Education and Social Care (HESC) Chamber. Some new rules came into force under the Tribunals, Courts and Enforcement Act 2007, which states that the Senior President of SEND has a duty to 'Have regard to the need for tribunals to be accessible, proceedings to be fair and handled quickly and effectively, and explore and develop innovative methods of resolving disputes'.

The HESC rules are intended to be 'Simple, flexible and easy to understand'. What this actually means for parents is that parties will no longer submit parallel case statements. This will be replaced by 'case management' whereby the parent will submit his case in writing and the LA will be required to respond within a given period of time. Other changes include a duty or requirement to cooperate with the tribunal and that a joint expert will only be appointed if both parties agree. The new case management system is to ensure that the right evidence is filed. This should reduce the number of tribunals that get cancelled at the last minute because of missing documents and should eradicate late evidence through the setting of a clear timetable which states the hearing date at the beginning of the process.

Other specific provisions include an exemption that all hearings should be made in public as well as the power to require a parent to make a child available for examination or assessment by an expert. There is also a similar power to require a school to allow a professional instructed by a parent into the school to assess the child's functioning in a school environment.

Case management will start very early in the process and this should enable the tribunal to consider fully what evidence and reports are needed to make a judgment. Advice and directives can then be issued to make sure that they are obtained prior to the hearing. It is to be hoped that this increase in negotiation will reduce the number of cases which have to be heard at tribunal, as well as the number of cases which are adjourned because of the panel's requirement for additional evidence.

Each case, under the new guidelines, will therefore involve either the issuing of standard paper directions, a preliminary hearing on the telephone or an oral hearing. These approaches will set out how each case will be managed, the key issues and evidence needed. If the Chair thinks that an oral hearing is necessary then this will be held at about ten weeks. If an oral hearing is deemed appropriate by the tribunal then both parties will be informed of the time and place that it will be held as well as of their right to attend. The intention is to provide initial scrutiny of most cases without having to attend an additional hearing. At preliminary hearings Chairs will sit alone rather than with a three-member panel which is also a change from the previous system.

Under the new system the tribunal can demand that evidence be released from the LA and will also have the power to order that the LA conduct assessments if necessary. In reality it is likely that the tribunal will know what the grounds for opposition are from the LA.

There has been a lot of conflicting information regarding the number of witnesses that are able to attend. This will be decided at the case management hearing. The rules state that any number can attend although it is highly unlikely that the tribunal would allow an unlimited number!

You can lodge an appeal to the First Tier Tribunal if:

- the LA refuses to carry out a Statutory Assessment or reassessment
- the LA refuses to issue a Statement
- the LA has made a Statement, or changed a Statement (you can appeal Part 2, 3 and/or 4)
- the LA refuses to change the school named on the Statement, if the Statement is at least a year old
- the LA decides to cease to maintain a Statement
- the LA decides not to change the Statement after reassessment.

Details of the procedure can be found on the SEND website.

You will have a two-month time limit to appeal to SEND from the date of the authority letter. That is the date stated upon it, not the date that you receive it. You can ask for an extension but you need to make sure that your grounds for doing this are clear.

You can register an appeal even if you don't have all of the documents required. The tribunal service will write to you after the submission of your case and request that you provide these within ten working days. As soon as your case is registered your LA will be informed. Your appeal will be registered within ten working days of receiving your request and you will be given the date of your appeal hearing as well as the date by which you must send all of the information to SEND. At this point you will be asked which expert witnesses you would like to attend.

The LA has to respond to SEND and to you within 30 days of receiving the information regarding your appeal. Sometimes the LA will concede at this point and give you what you want without further discussion. You can also withdraw your appeal. If the LA does not respond to SEND within the timeframe it may be barred from attending the appeal. If at this point you move house then your case will transfer to your new LA and it will take over the appeal as if it had made the judgments prior to appeal.

As stated previously, the new system outlines the process of case management; however, if your appeal goes to a tribunal hearing this will be heard by a legally qualified tribunal Chair and two specialist members who have knowledge and experience of children with SEN. At this hearing you can have representation from a solicitor although you cannot get legal aid for this. Many LAs now employ barristers to represent them at tribunal. You will receive a written decision as to the judgment and outcome of the hearing within ten working days of the tribunal. The LA must comply with this decision and there are timeframes to do so. The following list indicates how long complience should take:

- to undertake a Statutory Assessment or reassessment – four weeks

- to make a Statement – five weeks

- to change a Statement – five weeks

- to change a school named on a Statement – two weeks

- to continue a Statement or cancel a Statement – with immediate effect.

You have a right of further appeal if you feel that the decision is wrong in law, if things have changed substantially since the judgment or if you wish to have the decision set aside because of certain circumstances (for example, if a school cannot provide what it said it could). If you believe that a decision is wrong in law you also have a further right of appeal. This includes the tribunal not applying the correct law, making a procedural error, making a judgment with a lack of evidence or not giving adequate reasons for its decision. If a tribunal decides to set aside its decision (or part of it) then a further hearing will be held before a new ruling is made. You must seek permission from the First Tier Tribunal to appeal and this must be lodged within 28 days of the decision. Your appeal would be to the Administrative Appeals Chamber of the Upper Tribunal. This used to be the High Court but has changed under the new guidelines.

There have obviously been a number of cases which have further defined the law, and these can be significant when putting together a case for tribunal.

- Educational provision can encompass a wide range of activities depending on the level of disability that the child has. It may include a life-skills based curriculum where appropriate.

- Speech and language therapy should be considered as an educational need because of the impact that poor language and communication can have on learning; however, other therapeutic supports tend to be considered non educational needs. There is a case to consider that sensory integration therapy is an educational need for children with autism.

- There is no legal obligation for an LA to provide any sort of provision, however well stated, unless the child has a Statement of SEN.

- Provision should be specific and quantifiable.

- Ambiguous wording in Statements is unacceptable. This may include 'access to', 'as required', and so on. It should clearly state exactly what the provision is.

- Part 2 of the Statement should be written and considered before Part 3. It should not be undertaken the other way around. Once this has been decided then Part 4 can be considered.

- The LA remains legally obliged to make sure that the child receives the provision outlined in the Statement. It delegates this duty to schools but remains ultimately liable if this does not happen.

- There is a strengthened right to mainstream inclusion.

- Transport provided for a child must be non stressful. In real terms this usually means no longer than one hour each way from home to school.

- If a parental request for a specific school would amount to over-provision then it may be lawfully rejected. This is often referred to as seeking a 'Rolls Royce Service'.

- The provision required should meet the SEN outlined. SEND will rule only on matters of educational provision.

This obviously is not in any way a definitive list, and further help should be sought when preparing your case for tribunal. There are a number of specialist solicitors who deal with educational law and they would be best placed to advise you on engaging expert witnesses and putting together your case. I do not feel that it is appropriate for this book to make recommendations for this.

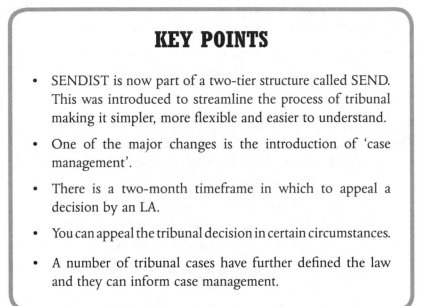

KEY POINTS

- SENDIST is now part of a two-tier structure called SEND. This was introduced to streamline the process of tribunal making it simpler, more flexible and easier to understand.

- One of the major changes is the introduction of 'case management'.

- There is a two-month timeframe in which to appeal a decision by an LA.

- You can appeal the tribunal decision in certain circumstances.

- A number of tribunal cases have further defined the law and they can inform case management.

Chapter 12

Transition

Transition can be really tough on young people with autism, causing very high anxiety. This can be due to a number of factors, particularly in a school environment. Sensory processing can be an issue, with the young person unable to make sense of the information he is presented with. Very busy environments, new smells and general hustle and bustle can all have an impact. The young person may not be able to draw on his own knowledge of what something new may look like or what it may entail and will need to be guided through this process. He may also feel vulnerable without the safety of known staff or family around him whom he trusts to support him.

Many pupils with autism find that as they become anxious they also become less able to communicate with others. Given the struggle that some may already have with social language and interaction it is easy to understand why they can feel uncomfortable when moving from one area to another. Transition is often given very little thought, and pre-planning is not always given the consideration that it requires.

Issues can be noted in a school environment when moving from one part of the building to another, or when moving from school to home. It is inevitable that young people with autism will have to manage transitions throughout their lives and it is imperative that they are properly prepared for this. Some of the following strategies can be useful for day-to-day transitions both in school and from school to home:

- A learning support assistant (LSA) or other pupils can act as a guide to establish routines of how to get from one area of the school to another. This can often be phased out over time.

- It can be useful to have a timetable or schedule stating which room a certain activity will happen in. For more able pupils this can take the form of a diary.

- The pupil should have a clear visual reminder of where he should be, what will happen, for how long, how he will know when he is finished and what he will be doing next.

- Initially photographs of the room layout and the member of staff can be useful particularly if a child is moving from a primary school (one in which the teacher stays with the class for most subjects) to a secondary school (one in which the pupils move rooms to subject specialists).

- If possible reduce the number of floor coverings and the number of thresholds that a pupil has to cross. This may not always be possible; however, supports should be in place to aid with this. Teach tolerance or remove the cause of the anxiety!

- Remember that the Disability Discrimination Act 2005 states that placements should not be accepted by parents or schools if adequate adaptations have not been made.

- Dual-purpose rooms such as the hall (e.g. for PE and lunch) can cause anxiety. Visual cues such as covering the tables with a tablecloth can be helpful to show the current purpose of the room.

- Buddy systems where the pupil with autism has other named pupils who will help them if they are unsure can be very helpful.

- Clear guidance should be offered during unstructured times such as break time and lunchtime.

- Pupils with autism often feel vulnerable if their backs are exposed as unexpected things can happen, so suggest they sit with their backs against a wall.

- Give the child with autism their own marked chair so that he does not have to make a choice about where to sit.

- On schedules, make sure it is clear that at the end of the day the child will go home.

- Mobile schedules can be useful to support a child transitioning to a taxi and then to home.

- If the journey is long give the child a favoured activity to engage with.

- Make sure that escorts have received some training about ASD so that they are able to respond effectively to issues which may arise during the journey.

- There must be support available during break times and lunchtimes, and access to common rooms must be allowed.

I would suggest that there is also a back-up plan of clear guidance as to what to do if the pupil becomes anxious or disorientated. This may be as simple as returning to the SENCO's office.

I have seen some innovative ways of supporting pupils with autism in their transition around buildings, such as colour-coded systems on walls leading the pupil to the correct department. Whatever is decided is best to support the process of transition is likely to have involved the consideration of the individual needs of the child, environmental factors (including staff responses and training) and visual supports.

Given how much support some young people will require with transition within a school it is easy to understand how transition from a school to a college would provoke severe anxiety without proper management. This can be compounded with issues of moving from child to adult services. There are likely to be a number of professionals involved in the transition to post 16 provision, and the process should begin at the Year 9 review. The Connexions Service will send a personal adviser to attend the review. These people have a particular responsibility to implement the transition plan for a young person with SEN which should be developed at the review and drawn up afterwards. The SEN Code of Practice states that a Connexions personal adviser must attend the Year 9 review whether or not that young person is in school.

The role and function of the Connexions adviser is to assist in the identification of the most appropriate post 16 provision. This decision should involve the young person wherever possible, as well as the parents, the school, the LA and social care. The plan developed at the Year 9 review should state the views of those involved in the decision and what has to happen before the following annual review. This may include the young person or the parents going to view provision.

The Disabled Persons Act 1986 places a statutory responsibility on social care to decide if a child is disabled and therefore eligible for an assessment for Adult Care Services. The Autism Act 2009 strengthens the case that there is a need and requirement to improve transition from child to adult services. Hopefully this will build upon legislation in Valuing People 2001 which states that effective links need to be in place within and between children's and adult services in both health and social care.

The SEN Code of Practice outlines the aims and purpose of a transition plan:

> The transition plan should draw together information from a range of individuals within and beyond school in order to plan coherently with the young person for their transition to adult life. The first plan should be completed following the annual review of the statement held in year 9 and updated at least on an annual basis. The aim of the annual review in year 9 and subsequent years is to review the young person's statement (and) draw up and subsequently review the transition plan.

The underlying principles for everyone involved should ensure that the process is participative, holistic, supportive, evolving, inclusive and collaborative. The guidance would certainly indicate that this should be a fluid document which captures the future needs of a young person. Information should be made available to parents from the LA prior to the Year 9 transition review.

The Year 9 review

The aim of this meeting is to review the Statement and draw up the transition plan. The meeting MUST involve a Connexions adviser and the head teacher MUST invite the following people: the child's parents, a relevant teacher, an LA representative, a Connexions adviser, any person that the LA specifies and any other person that the head teacher considers appropriate. Dependent on the pupil's needs, the head teacher should invite the pupil, an LA educational psychologist, a Health Service representative and any other professionals who are closely involved.

The Connexions adviser should have met with the young person prior to the review and started to ascertain his views and wishes for the future using Record of Achievement or Progress files. The Connexions adviser will use the Connexions Assessment Profile to provide a snapshot of the young person's life and situation at a particular point. This should involve assessing the impact that a SEN may have on a young person's life and should also include strengths and needs.

A draft should be circulated following the Year 9 review meeting and this must be framed in a way that supports continuous monitoring and review, including clear outcomes. After the Year 9 review the Connexions adviser will stay in contact with the young person to continue dialogue and development in a meaningful way. The school should also be supporting the young person's specific curriculum needs during this process. In reality the regularity and timeframe of this can be vague. Once the transition plan has been drafted and agreed, arrangements should include the new post 16 provider.

The Year 10 review

This should provide an opportunity to look at assessment, planning, implementation and review and update any goals. There should be feedback on progress to all agencies and ongoing discussion regarding curriculum to support the plan.

The Year 11 review

The Connexions adviser should offer advice regarding likely post 16 provision in light of the plan. This will have been discussed at previous reviews. Any arrangements surrounding the collation of information about appropriate post 16 provision should be outlined here, including any necessary arrangements for transition.

Some students will require a lengthy transition into post 16 provision. This may include developing a book of photographs of the environment including outside areas, a map of the provision, key staff with whom they will be working and any other relevant information.

It may be that the potential student visits the site a number of times to familiarise himself with the layout. The first visit may simply be about giving the student an understanding of the length of the journey and an opportunity to view the outside of the building. A portfolio of information can be collated for the young person and this can act as his aide memoire when he begins full time.

Many students have benefited from visits which extend in duration starting with 30 minutes and building to a whole day to expose the young person slowly to new systems and routines. This should also include debriefing sessions to resolve any issues and talk about any worries or concerns.

It should be noted that for some students the anxiety of moving to a new provision can be so overwhelming that it may be in their interests to be informed of the move the day that it happens rather than put them through months of stress. This will only be true of a small number of very complex young people, but it serves as a reminder that all transition planning should be led by the needs of the young person. There is a very good toolkit available to support young people with autism moving from primary to secondary provision and this which was developed in a pilot project could easily be modified to use at post 16. It can be found on the Autism Spectrum Disorder transition toolkit website (www.autismtoolkit.com).

The Education and Skills Act 2008 gave LAs statutory responsibility to make arrangements for the assessment of young people with a learning disability regarding their post 16 placement. This is known as an S139A and forms a singular assessment which can take over from a Statement of SEN, although it is not mandatory to have a Statement for this to happen. The statutory guidance states that when an LA believes that an assessment would benefit the learner it will arrange for one to take place. The S139A can replace a Statement but does not have to do so. A Statement has more legal recourse and it may be beneficial to retain it.

Many agencies opt out of supporting young people with poor communication skills citing the fact that they have not expressed an opinion as to what they want or need. Parents can apply for a 'Deputyship' which is a form of power of attorney and this will give them the right to advocate for their child. This application has to be done before the child's 18th birthday to the Court of Protection and will cost approximately £400. If you are unwaged it will be free. Further details can be found on the Direct.Gov website.

Progression through Partnerships (DfES, Department of Health and Department for Work and Pensions 2007) describes a joint approach to supporting a young person to allow him to access the education that he wants and needs. This should be taken into account when assessing and planning the transition of young people with disabilities.

Furthermore, the LA should establish good provision and support and give priority to these young people who are considered to be not in employment, education or training (NEET) (or those at risk of becoming NEET).

These directives give further guidance to LAs about their duties to young people at post 16, specifically if they have a disability. It is useful to have a full understanding of the implications of these, and how effective support can be secured.

KEY POINTS

- Transition around a school or from home to school can be the source of much anxiety for a young person with autism. He may need strategies to support him through this.

- Transition from school to college can also be a very stressful time. A clear plan should be developed and implemented by a range of professionals starting at the Year 9 annual review.

- At post 16 the LA has statutory responsibilities to assess young people with learning disabilities to ensure access to education and support.

Chapter 13

Brothers and Sisters

There are many issues to consider when examining the impact of an autistic child on a brother or sister. The impact can be hugely variable and certainly will be different in each family setting. It does not, however, follow that the higher functioning the child the less impact there is. I have worked with a number of families who have really struggled to balance the needs of all the children in the family and there is no formula or easy answer for achieving this balance. At the outset, it appears to be simple; inform all the family about the issues posed by a child with an ASD and everyone will then know how best to work with the situation. However, things can become complicated when young people are not told about their diagnosis; in fact some do not have a diagnosis and families do not seek one out. This can be for a number of very valid reasons such as not being labelled or fear of other people's responses. This is a debate which is far reaching and complex and it will be for you and your family to talk about this issue and make a judgement. There is no right or wrong, although there have been some accounts from young people with autism who express relief at being informed why they are 'different'.

Schools are getting better at implementing programmes of whole-school awareness, not just amongst staff members, and this has led to greater global understanding of the condition. Many establishments are now offering buddy and mentoring schemes as well as using circle time to explore issues which children may find difficult to understand and to outline how young people can support each other in a truly inclusive manner. This is all a huge step in the right direction, and it can only be a good thing; however, the impact that a child with autism can have on a sibling is significant and will need to be discussed and addressed by the family and the school, particularly if the sibling attends the same school.

The issues can be exacerbated if the young person receives no short breaks, or support from outside agencies. I have worked with families who have self-funded carers and helpers not only to support their child with autism but also to facilitate activities with other siblings. It is important that the needs of other siblings are not overshadowed by the child with autism and that everyone has opportunities to engage in activities that they enjoy. The reality of achieving this can be difficult, but nonetheless it is something that we should be striving for.

The following are some of the issues that have been raised with me by children living with a sibling with autism and some of the ways that you may address these. It may be appropriate to consider how modifications to family life can be made which suit everyone. This is a tough balance and there will be some things that you are unable to compromise on without causing huge distress to the child with autism.

All the furniture in the lounge is pushed back against the walls and is kept clear to reduce the chances of objects being disturbed or damaged.

If at all possible make sure that siblings have access to areas which are comfortable and welcoming, especially when their friends come to the house. If this is not possible, it may be that you can make an area in their bedroom that can act as a small lounge area for them.

The cupboard doors in the kitchen are locked because of food intolerances.

Dedicate a cupboard to other children and make sure that this has food in there that they like, including special treats. It could still be kept locked and they could have a key.

The bedrooms of siblings have to be kept clear or things get broken.

It should be an absolute given that bedrooms are private spaces and that no one goes in unless invited. This should be true of all bedrooms and if star locks are required then fit them (star locks are used extensively in schools as it is easy and inexpensive to purchase multiple keys).

Siblings cannot sleep because of the noise from an autistic brother or sister.

Provide ear plugs for siblings and look at soundproofing devices which can block out unwanted noise. Low-level music via an mp3 player can also work to block out noise.

The TV and/or computer is dominated by the child with autism.

Agree times that each child can access the television and computer and make a timetable which is adhered to. A television elsewhere can alleviate issues but again if this is not possible then parameters around who can watch television and when are useful.

Activities out of the house are limited for siblings because they are not appropriate for your child with autism.

Sometimes it may be a case of divide and conquer! If you have a partner then splitting the children so that they can engage in different activities can be very helpful. Friends and family can also be extremely useful in this capacity.

Often siblings can think that things are unfair as displays of behaviour that would be unacceptable by them are accepted.

This is where it becomes vital to explain the basis of behaviours to siblings and that their brother or sister is not just being naughty, rather they are unable to cope with the anxiety that they are feeling.

It is likely that you will need to be extremely creative to solve some of these issues and that you may have to resort to radical solutions! I know of one family who split their house in half and mum lived in one half with their son with autism whilst the other children lived in the other half with dad. Whilst I am not suggesting that you segregate your family, sometimes it is about organising the home environment in an entirely different way. It is important that you acknowledge the stress that an autistic child can place upon a family unit and look for solutions which support everyone.

It may also be worth contacting your local autistic society as many of them have resources which can help siblings to understand what autism means and why people with autism respond in the way that they do. Some also run sibling groups and days, which can be a great source of support. There is a wealth of literature available written by people with autism who give accounts of their lives and how they perceive the world. This can be really useful to share with siblings. A list of some of the literature available can be found in the Useful Websites and Suggested Further Reading section at the end of the book. Siblings can become great ambassadors for people with autism if they are given the means to do so.

Extended family members can be a great help in sharing childcare and therefore enabling all of the children to have positive experiences and fun. This can be especially helpful to split the children who want to undertake different activities. However, there may be issues with understanding your child with autism and it will be important that any adult taking responsibility has an understanding of the specific needs of the child. Any special diets should be clearly shared with the adult. It may be easier actually to provide the food required rather than risk a child being given food to which he is intolerant. It will also be important that the carer understands the behaviours of your child and the likely response to situations. Finally, it will also be vital that the carer understands what to do if things don't go to plan. These are things that I am sure you would share with someone taking charge of your child; however, if you are highly stressed and lacking sleep, and relieved that finally you are going to have a couple of hours to yourself it may be that you omit to give this detail.

Any family member undertaking care should understand the reasons behind the approaches that you use so that they are able to modify them slightly if required. Finally, do not feel that you are alone. Often family members and friends want to help but don't want to feel like they are being intrusive and think that they lack the knowledge and understanding to care for a child with autism. Take time to share your child with them and help them to get to know and understand the unique nature of children with autism. It can be very hard to deal with the day-to-day issues when you are caring for a child with autism as well as other siblings. Take time to work together and to celebrate the achievements of all members of the family.

KEY POINTS

- It is important that there is a balance maintained between meeting the needs of a child with an ASD and those of his siblings.

- Schools can be pivotal in raising awareness and understanding of young people with autism.

- There are common issues which are frequently raised by brothers and sisters of children with ASD which will need to be considered.

- There is likely to be a range of services and support available from your local autistic society which may include relevant literature and sibling (brother and sister) groups.

Chapter 14

Frequently Asked Questions

These are questions that are frequently posed when talking to parent groups. I hope that they are of some use to you.

Can parents cause autism?

The myth of 'refrigerator parents' was created by Bruno Bettelheim in 1967. This has been found to have no basis at all. Autism is not caused by faulty or inadequate parenting. The only link between parents and autism is likely to be genetic.

Is autism always characterised by special or savant skills?

It is a myth that all people with autism have savant skills. Less than 10 per cent of individuals with autism will have superior skills or abilities.

Do children grow out of autism?

Autism tends to persist into adulthood. Early intervention would seem to be the key to reducing the effect that an ASD can have on an individual, and effective support and programmes can increase skills. There have been claims of 'cures'; however, none that have been proven. With age, it is usually harder to detect the autism as the person has learned strategies to deal with difficult situations and has chosen a lifestyle that suits his autism.

Which medical treatments work best?

There are no specific medical treatments available for ASD, although a number of drugs are used to treat the symptoms of anxiety and sleep difficulties. These should be very carefully monitored and should not be used to 'manage' behaviour. There have been a number of claims of improvement through casein-, gluten- and dairy-free diets; however, these have been unsubstantiated. Your GP should be able to advise further.

How do I get a Statement for child who is post 16?

A Statement can be sought for any child under the age of 18. This Statement forms the basis of setting out his specific educational needs and how these are to be addressed and is enforceable by law. You may wish to consider the length of this process prior to attempting to get a Statement post 16 as this document ceases to be enforceable at 19.

How do I get LSC funding?

Some colleges and post 16 provisions used to be funded by the LSC. What this effectively means is that the LA does not fund the child, rather all the funds used to come from the LSC. By accepting LSC funding the child's Statement is no longer valid at post 16. The LSC has now disbanded and has been replaced by the Young People's Learning Agency (YPLA).

If my child is not coping in school, should I withdraw him?

If your child is having problems at school, try to work with the school to seek solutions. If your child has a Statement and you decide to remove him from school, you are agreeing to take on the responsibility for his educational provision. Unless you plan to home school your child, withdrawing him tends to be unproductive in terms of securing appropriate provision for the future.

At what stage should I have independent assessments done?

You may require independent assessments on your child if the LA refuses to issue a Statement or if the Statement does not reflect the child's needs. Some parents have these assessments done prior to going to tribunal as evidence of need.

My child has huge difficulties at home yet the school says he's fine and that it could be down to parenting. How do I address this?

It is often the case that children behave better at school and are very challenging at home. This is not because their parents are poor at understanding and managing them. Home may be the only part of the day where they can relax and be themselves. It may be because of the great effort needed at school in trying to fit in and do the right thing that they are exhausted when they arrive home and need to release the tension and stresses of the day. Try to involve experts at the school or elsewhere to help with problems at home. Be clear about what the issues are and the outcomes that you would like. Request social care involvement, and try to join a support group as there will be a number of parents who have had to tackle similar issues. The NAS helpline can give advice to parents on these types of issues (Tel: 0845 070 4004).

Should I involve social care?

Make social care aware if you are struggling, as you may require support from them in the future. Social care professionals can help with pointing you in the right direction for information. Sometimes educational placement can be part funded by social care, although the LA will negotiate this on your behalf.

I currently live abroad but will be moving back to England. Where do I start?

As soon as you know where you are going to live you will need to involve the LA. It is likely that if your child has significant SEN a meeting will be arranged to discuss the options available. Even if you are looking for a specialist school that is not under the management of the LA you will still need to contact the LA as it will be responsible for the fees.

My child has a Statement of SEN and I'm moving county. What happens to his current or future placement?

The county that you move to will then become responsible for any fees for current provision. The new LA is likely to make its own assessment as its provision will differ from the old LA and it needs to make its own decisions on provision in light of that. It may undertake another Statutory Assessment to update the Statement. Any future placements will also be funded by the LA or the YPLA, formerly known as the LSC.

Does autism run in families?

There is some evidence to suggest that you are more likely to have another child with autism if you already have one (the increased risk is estimated at about 2 or 3 per cent).

Does a restricted diet have any impact on children with autism?

Some children with autism restrict their own diet and eat a very limited range of foods and may drink only certain fluids. Parents can worry about the health implications. Most children do not appear to suffer in terms of height and weight gain. Individuals with autism may also eat on a very irregular basis. Some children suffer from severe constipation which can clearly affect their well-being and mood. It is useful to get the advice of a dietician if you have any worries about your child's diet.

Should my child with autism attend a mainstream school so that he has better role models?

Inclusion should be the preferred option as a given; however, your child needs to be understood and provided with appropriate and adequate support. If you feel your child can thrive (rather than just cope) in a mainstream setting then it should be the option that you take.

Does the triple measles, mumps and rubella (MMR) vaccine cause autism?

There is no proof to suggest that this is true although some parents believe it to be so. If you are worried then it may be worth considering single vaccines, although these can be expensive.

Glossary

AAC	Augmentative and alternative communication
ABA	Applied Behaviour Analysis
ACE	Advisory Centre for Education
ADHC	Aiming High for Disabled Children
ADHD	Attention deficit hyperactivity disorder
ADI	Autism Diagnostic Interview
ADOS	Autism Diagnostic Observation Schedule
AIT	Auditory Integration Therapy
AOSI	Autism Observation Scale for Infants
AS	Asperger syndrome
ASD	Autism spectrum disorder
BESD	Behavioural, emotional and social disabilities
CaF	Contact a Family
CAF	Common Assessment Framework
CAMHS	Child and Adolescent Mental Health Services
CARS	Childhood Autism Rating Scale
CQC	Care Quality Commission
CRB	Criminal Records Bureau
CSCI	Commission for Social Care Inspection
CYPP	Children and Young People's Plan
DCSF	Department for Children, Schools and Families
DfES	Department for Education and Skills

DH	Department of Health
DISCO	Diagnostic Interview for Social and Communication Disorders
DSM	Diagnostic and Statistical Manual
ECM	*Every Child Matters*
G and T	Gifted and talented
GDA	General development assessment
GP	General practitioner
HESC	Health, Education and Social Care (Chamber)
HFA	High-functioning autism
ICD	International Classification of Diseases
IDP	Inclusion Development Programme
IEP	Individual Education Plan
IPSEA	Independent Parental Special Education Advice
LA	Local Authority (formerly known as Local Education Authority, LEA)
LAC	Looked after child
LD	Learning difficulties
LSA	Learning support assistant
LSC	Learning and Skills Council
M-CHAT	Modified Checklist for Autism in Toddlers
MLD	Moderate learning difficulties
MMR	Measles, mumps and rubella
NAPC	National Autism Plan for Children
NAS	National Autistic Society
NATSPEC	Association of National Specialist Colleges
NC	National Curriculum

NEET	Not in employment, education or training
OCD	Obsessive compulsive disorder
OAASIS	Office for Advice, Assistance, Support and Information on Special Needs
Ofsted	Office for Standards in Education
OT	Occupational therapist, occupational therapy
PD	Physical disabilities
PDA	Pathological demand avoidance
PDD (NOS)	Pervasive developmental disorder (not otherwise specified)
PECS	Picture Exchange Communication System
PEDS	Parents' Evaluation of Developmental Status
PMLD	Profound and multiple learning difficulties
SaLT	Speech and language therapy, speech and language therapist
SCQ	Social Communication Questionnaire
SEN	Special educational need(s)
SENCO	Special educational needs coordinator
SEND	Special educational needs and disability tribunal (formerly SENDIST)
SLD	Severe learning difficulties
SpLD	Specific learning difficulties (dyslexia)
SULP	Social Use of Language Programme
TAC	Team Around the Child
TEACCH	Treatment and Education of Autistic and related Communication-handicapped Children
YPLA	Young People's Learning Agency

References

American Academy of Pediatrics (2007) 'What are the early warning signs of autism?' *Science Daily*, 29 October. Available at www.sciencedaily.com/releases/2007/10/07102912047.htm, accessed on 4 September 2010.

American Psychiatric Association (1994) *Diagnostic and Statistical Manual of Mental Health Disorders* (Fourth edition). Washington, DC: American Psychiatric Association.

Asperger, H. (1944) *Autistic Psychopathology in Childhood*. Cited in U. Frith (ed.) (1989) *Autism and Asperger Syndrome*. Cambridge: Cambridge University Press.

Baron-Cohen, S., Scott, F.J., Allison, C., Williams, J. *et al.* (2009) 'Prevalence of autism-spectrum conditions: UK school-based population study.' *The British Journal of Psychiatry 194*, 500–209.

Baron-Cohen, S., Wheelwright, S., Cox, A., Baird, G., Charmen, T., Swettenham, J., Drew, A. and Doehring, P. (2000) 'The early identification of autism: The Checklist for Autism in Toddlers (CHAT).' *Journal of the Royal Society of Medicine 93*, 521–525.

Bondy, A.S. and Frost, L.A. (1994) 'The Delaware Autistic Program.' In S.L. Harris and J.S. Handleman (eds) *Preschool Education Programs for Children with Autism*. Austin, TX: Pro-Ed.

Bryson, S.E., Zwaigenbaum, L., McDermott, C., Rombough, V. and Brian, J. (2008) 'The Autism Observation Scale for Infants: Scale development and reliability data.' *Journal of Autism and Developmental Disorders 38*, 731–738.

Christie, P., Newson, E., Prevezer, W. and Chandler, S. *First Steps in Intervention with Your Child with Autism: Frameworks for Communication*. London: Jessica Kingsley Publishers.

Dawson, G. and Osterling, J. (1997) Early Intervention in Autism.' In M. Guralnick (ed.) *The Effectiveness of Early Intervention*. Baltimore, MD: Brookes Publishing Co., Inc.

DCSF (Department for Children, Schools and Families) (2010) *The Lamb Report. Special Educational Needs and Parental Confidence*. London: The Stationery Office.

DfES (Department for Education and Skills) (2001) *Special Educational Needs Code of Practice*. London: The Stationery Office.

DfES, Department of Health and Department for Work and Pensions (2007) *Progression through Partnership*. London: HMSO.

Glascoe, F.P., Maclean, W.E. and Stone, W.L. (1991) 'The importance of parents' concerns about their child's behaviour.' *Clinical Pediatrics (Philadelphia) 30*, 1, 8–11, discussion 12–14.

Happé, F. and Frith, U. (2009) 'The beautiful otherness of the autistic mind.' *Philosophical Transactions of the Royal Society 364*, 1522, 1345–1350.

Johnson, C.P., Myers, S.M. and the Council on Children with Disabilities (2007) 'Identification and evaluation of children with autism spectrum disorders.' *Pediatrics 120*, 5, 1183–1215.

Jordan, R., Jones, G. and Murray, D. (1998) *Educational Interventions for Children with Autism. A Literature Review of Recent and Current Practice*. London and Birmingham: Department for Education and Employment and the University of Birmingham.

Kanner, L. (1943) 'Autistic disturbance of affective contact.' *Nervous Child 2*, 217–250.

Kaufman, B. (1976) *To Love is to be Happy With*. London: Souvenir Press.

Le Couteur, A., Lord, C. and Rutter, M. (2003) *The Autism Diagnostic Interview-Revised (ADI-R)*. Los Angeles, CA: Western Psychological Services.

Leekam, S.R., Libby, S.J., Wing, L., Gould, J. and Taylor, C. (2002) 'The Diagnostic Interview for Social and Communication Disorders: Algorithms for ICD-10 childhood autism.' *Journal of Child Psychology and Psychiatry and Allied Disciplines 43*, 3, 327–342.

Lord, C., Risi, S., Lambrecht, L., Cook, E.H. Jr, Leventhal, B.L., DiLavore, P. *et al.* (2000) 'The Autism Diagnostic Observation Schedule – generic: A standard measure of social and communication deficits associated with the spectrum of autism.' *Journal of Autism and Developmental Disorders 30*, 3, 205–223.

Murray, D. (ed.) (2006) *Coming Out Asperger: Diagnosis, Disclosure, and Self-Confidence*. London: Jessica Kingsley Publishers.

NIASA (National Initiative for Autism: Screening and Assessment) (2003) *National Autism Plan for Children (NAPC): Plan for the Identification, Assessment, Diagnosis and Access to Early Interventions for Pre-school and Primary School-aged Children with Autism Spectrum Disorders*. London: The National Autistic Society.

Nind, M. and Hewett, D. (2005) *Access to Communication: Developing the Basics of Communication with People with Severe Learning Difficulties through Intensive Interaction (2nd edition)*. London: David Fulton.

Parsons, S., Guildberg, K., Macleod, A., Jones, G., Prunty, A. and Balfe, T. (2009) *International Review of the Literature of Evidence of Best Practice Provision in the Education of Persons with Autistic Spectrum Disorders*. Trim: NCSE.

Rinaldi, W. (1995) *The Social Use of Language Programme (Primary and Pre- School Teaching Pack)*. Windsor: NFER.

Rogers, S.J., Herbison, J., Lewis, H., Pantone, J. and Reis, K. (1986) 'An approach for enhancing the symbolic, communicative and interpersonal functioning of young children with autism and severe emotional handicaps.' *Journal of the Division for Early Childhood 10*, 135–148.

Rutter, M., Bailey, A. and Lord, C. (2003) *SCQ: Social Communication Questionnaire*. Los Angeles, CA: Western Psychological Services. (Previously known as *The Manual for the SCQ*.)

Schopler, E., Reichler, R.J. and Renner B.R. (1988) *CARS (The Childhood Autism Rating Scales)*. Los Angeles, CA: Western Psychological Services.

Squires, J., Bricker, D. with Twombly, E., Nickel, R., Clifford, J., Murphy, K., Hoselton, R., Potter, L., Mounts, L. and Farrell, J. (2009) *Ages and Stages Questionnaires (Third edition) (ASQ-3): A Parent-completed Child-monitory System*. Baltimore. Brookes Publishing Co., Inc.

Terrance, H.S. (1963) 'Discrimination learning with and without "error".' *Journal of the Experimental Analysis of Behavior 6*, 1–27.

Whitaker, P., Barratt, P., Joy, H., Potter, M. and Thomas, G. (1998) 'Children with autism and peer group support: Using circle of friends.' *British Journal of Special Education 25*, 2, 60–64.

Wing, L., Leekam, S.R., Libby, S.J., Gould, J. and Larcombe, M. (2002) 'The Diagnostic Interview for Social and Communication Disorders: Background, inter-rater reliability and clinical use.' *Journal of Child Psychology and Psychiatry and Allied Disciplines 43*, 3, 307–325.

WHO (World Health Organization) (1993) *Mental Disorders: A Glossary and Guide to Their Classification in Accordance with the 10th Revision of the International Classification of Diseases (ICD-10)*. Geneva: WHO.

Useful Websites and Suggested Further Reading

Useful websites

Websites on specific topics relating to autism, strategy and legislation

A Home Education
Website www.ahomeeducation.co.uk
This site contains further details about requirements of home schooling as well as advice for lessons and planning.

Advisory Centre for Education (ACE)
www.ace-ed.org.uk
Template letter to request a Statutory Assessment.

Aiming High for Disabled Children (AHDC)
www.dcsf.gov.uk/everychildmatters/healthandwellbeing/ahdc
Information about the AHDC agenda.

Autism-Spectrum Quotient (ASQ) Test
www.wired.com/wired/archive/9.12/aqtest.html
This is a free online test developed by Simon Baron-Cohen and colleagues to measure autism in adults.

Autism Spectrum Disorder transition toolkit
www.autismtoolkit.com
Guidance on transition, including a pupil transition workbook which can be downloaded free of charge.

AutismWeb™
www.autismweb.com
Includes information on restricted diets and their effectiveness.

British Dyslexia Association
Tel: 0845 251 9002
www.bdadyslexia.org.uk

Contact a Family
Tel: 0808 808 3555
www.cafamily.org.uk
This organisation provides details of all national support groups for childhood disorders and syndromes.

Department for Education Inclusion Development Programme on the Autistic Spectrum. Resource for all mainstream primary and secondary schools
www.nationalstrategies.standards.dcsf.gov.uk/sen
Follow the link to the Inclusion Development Programme (IDP). Click on 'Autism' for a checklist to produce a sensory profile and a school effectiveness checklist.

DCSF EduBase
www.edubase.gov.uk
This site has a list of all schools in the country.

Directgov: Government, citizens and rights
www.direct.gov.uk/en/governmentcitizensandrights/Mentalcapacityandthelaw/
Makingarrangementsincaseyoulosementalcapacity/DG_176235
This site offers advice on making an application to the Court of Protection for deputyship.

Dyspraxia Foundation
Tel: 01462 454 986
www.dyspraxiafoundation.org.uk

Education Otherwise
www.education-otherwise.org.uk
Provides useful information for families who home tutor.

Gabbitas
www.gabbitas.co.uk
This is where you can purchase the Gabbitas Guide to *Schools for Special Needs*.

Good Practice Guidance for Autistic Spectrum Disorders
www.teachernet.gov.uk/wholeschool/sen/asds/asdgoodpractice/

HANEN
www.hanen.org
This site offers home-based communication programmes for infants and juniors with autism.

Independent Schools Council
www.isc.co.uk
This site offers a search facility for a school.

Independent Special Boarding International
www.isbi.com
This site offers information on independent specialist schools.

LOVAAS Institute
www.lovaas.com
This site gives information on intensive ABA programmes for children.

Makaton®
www.makaton.org
This site provides a language programme offering a structured, multi-modal approach for the teaching of communication, language and literacy skills.

The National Autistic Society (NAS)
Tel: 0845 070 4004
www.nas.org.uk
This organisation provides a wealth of information on all aspects of services for people with autism and their families.

National Parent Partnership Network (NPPN)
www.parentpartnership.org.uk
This site gives details about local Parent Partnership Services (PPS).

Office for Advice, Assistance, Support and Information on Special Needs (OAASIS)
www.oaasis.co.uk
This site has useful free information leaflets including what to look for when choosing an independent specialist school.

Office for Standards in Education (Ofsted)
www.ofsted.gov.uk/reports
This is the link to the Ofsted reports of all schools.

Pathological Demand Avoidance Syndrome (PDA) Contact Group Forum Board
http://ccgi.pdacontact.org.uk/forum/
A forum to ask questions and discuss PDA with other parents and professionals.

Peach (Parents for the Early intervention of Autism in Children)
www.peach.org.uk
A charity which supports parents who wish to use ABA programmes with children.

Qualifications and Curriculum Development Agency
www.qcda.gov.uk/curriculum/80.aspx
This site has frequently asked questions regarding inclusion and SEN.

Research Autism
www.researchautism.net/interventionitem.ikml?ra=38
Follow the link for information on Daily Life Therapy.

Schoolsnet
www.schoolsnet.com
This site offers information on independent specialist schools.

SEN Code of Practice 2001
www.teachernet.gov.uk/wholeschool/sen/sencodeintro
This link will take you to a downloadable copy of the SEN Code of Practice.

Steiner Schools
www.steiner.edu
This site gives information on the Steiner philosophy.

Treatment and Education of Autistic and Communication-related Handicapped Children (TEACCH)
www.teacch.com
This site offers information on the TEACCH approach.

Widgit
www.widgit.com
This site provides symbols and products to support AAC.

Agencies who can support parents through the Statementing process and SEND tribunals

Education Equality
www.educationalequality.co.uk

Independent Parental Special Education Advice (IPSEA)
www.ipsea.org.uk

Network 81
www.network81.org

Rathbone
www.rathboneuk.org

Special Educational Needs and Disability Tribunals Service (SEND)
www.sendist.gov.uk
For details on how to appeal a decision made by your LA regarding your child.

SOS!SEN
www.sossen.org.uk

Websites with general information on autism spectrum disorders

www.autismconnect.org.uk
www.autism-awareness.org.uk
http://aspergersyndrome.org
www.autism-resources.com
www.autismuk.com
www.lookingupautism.org
www.mugsy.org

Suggested further reading

Textbooks and publications

Attwood, T. (1997) *Asperger Syndrome: A Guide for Parents and Professionals*. London: Jessica Kingsley Publishers.

Baron-Cohen, S. and Bolton, P. (2002) *Autism: The Facts*. Oxford: Oxford University Press.

Christie, P., Newson, E., Newson, J. and Prevexer, W. (1992) 'An Interactive Language and Communication for Nonspeaking Children.' In D. A. Lane and A. Miller, *Child and Adolescent Therapy: A Handbook*. Buckingham: Open University Press.

Dawson, G. and Osterling, J. (1997) 'Early Intervention in Autism.' In M. Guralnick *The Effectiveness of Early Intervention*. Baltimore, MD: Brookes Publishing.

DfES (Department for Education and Skills) (2002) *Autistic Spectrum Disorders: Good Practice Guidance*. London: DfES Publications.

Howlin, P. (1998) *Children with Autism and Asperger Syndrome*. London: Wiley.

Jones, G. (2002) *Educational Provision for Children with Autism and Asperger Syndrome*. London: David Fulton.

Jordan, R. (2001) *Autism with Severe Learning Difficulties*. London: Souvenir Press.

Jordan, R. and Jones, G. (1999) *Meeting the Needs of Children with an Autistic Spectrum Disorder*. London: David Fulton.

Jordan, R. and Powell, S. (1995) *Understanding and Teaching Children with Autism*. Chichester: Wiley.

Kaufman, B. (1976) *To Love is to be Happy With*. London: Souvenir Press.

NAS (National Autistic Society, The) (2001) *Approaches to Autism. An Easy-to-use Guide to Many and Varied Approaches to Autism*. London: NAS.

Natspec (Association of National Specialist Colleges) 'COPE' directory of post 16 residential education for young people with special needs, available from Orca Book Services, Tel: 01202 665432.

Natspec Annual Directory of Members and Associated Colleges, available from Janice Biggs, Natspec Administrator, Tel: 020 8471 3284; Queen Alexandra College, Tel: 0121 428 5050; Portland College, Tel: 01623 499111; Derwen College, Tel: 01691 661234.

Nind, M. and Hewett, D. (2005) *Access to Communication: Developing the Basics of Communication with People with Severe Learning Difficulties through Intensive Interaction (2nd edition)*. London: David Fulton.

Osman, B. B. (1997) *Learning Disabilities and ADHD: A Family Guide to Living and Learning Together*. New York: Wiley.

Rogers, S. J., Herbison, J., Lewis, H., Pantone, J. and Reis, K. (1986) 'An approach for enhancing the symbolic, communicative and interpersonal functioning of young children with autism and severe emotional handicaps.' *Journal of the Division for Early Childhood 10*, 135–148.

Wing, L. (1996) *The Autistic Spectrum*. London: Constable.

Acts of Parliament (England and Wales)

Disabled Persons Act 1986

Disability Discrimination Act 1995

Education Act 1996

Human Rights Act 1998

Special Educational Needs and Disability Act 2001

Disability Discrimination Act 2005

Education and Skills Act 2008
Autism Act 2009

Personal accounts of autism

Grandin, T. (1995) *Thinking in Pictures and Other Reports from My Life with Autism.* New York: Doubleday.

Lawson, W. (2001) *Life Behind Glass. A Personal Account of Autism Spectrum Disorder.* London: Jessica Kingsley Publishers.

Sainsbury, C. (2002) *Martian in the Playground. Understanding the Schoolchild with Asperger Syndrome.* London: Lucky Duck.

Tammet, D. (2006) *Born on a Blue Day.* London: Hodder & Stoughton.

Williams, D. (1992) *Nobody Nowhere.* New York: Time Books.

Films about people with autism

Rain Man (1998) Directed by Barry Levinson. United States: United Artists.

Snow Cake (2006) Directed by Marc Evans. Canada/United Kingdom: Revolution Films/Rhombus Media/UK Film Council.

Index